SOUTH
to
SELMA

'Outside Agitators' and the
Civil Rights March that
Changed

GARY G. YERKEY

GK Press
Washington, D.C.

GK Press

P.O. Box 11816
Washington, D.C. 20008

ISBN-10: 1484868951
ISBN-13: 9781484868959
Library of Congress Control Number: 2013908764
CreateSpace Independent Publishing Platform
North Charleston, South Carolina

In Memory of Jerry Thompson
(1923-2010)

CONTENTS

Preface.. vii

CHAPTER 1: The Telegram 1

CHAPTER 2: "Good-Natured Louts".................................13

CHAPTER 3: Protesting the Protests.................................23

CHAPTER 4: "A Sad Waste of Time" 33

CHAPTER 5: Covering the "Race Beat" 39

CHAPTER 6: The Clergy Heeds the Call 47

CHAPTER 7: The Trouble with Success 57

CHAPTER 8: A Sea of Mud.................................67

CHAPTER 9: Anger Turned to Good.................................77

CHAPTER 10: Stars Come Out for Freedom 83

CHAPTER 11: Loving the Hell Out of Alabama 87

CHAPTER 12: Too Many People Just Talking...................93

CHAPTER 13: A Heroic Christian Deed 97

CHAPTER 14: Nonviolence Runs Out 107

EPILOGUE 113

Bibliography...119

Index...125

Notes 133

PREFACE

It was as close to the Reverend Martin Luther King Jr.—and to history in the making—as I would ever get, that bright Sunday morning in Alabama nearly fifty years ago.

A spellbinding orator, he would not disappoint. "You will be the people that will light a new chapter in the history books of our nation," he told us at the start of what would become the most celebrated civil rights march in US history. "Walk together, children. Don't you get weary, and it will lead us to the Promised Land. And Alabama will be a new Alabama, and America will be a new America."

It was heady stuff, to be sure, his voice rising as he told us we would be serving a cause greater than ourselves, which to me, at least, was something of a new idea.

Now some fifty years later, I am still at a loss to explain what drew me to Selma. I would like say it was the cause being pursued—nothing more, nothing less. Mentors like the Reverend Jerry Thompson, then chaplain at Ripon College in Wisconsin where I was a student, certainly played a pivotal role. Others did as well. It could have been something in the 1960s air. Or it could have been the pull of escaping the lingering Wisconsin winter for the warmer Deep South.

Representative John Lewis (D) of Georgia, chairman of the Student Nonviolent Coordinating Committee (SNCC) at the time, told me on a recent return visit to Selma that in his view, the march, which began in Selma on Sunday, March 21, 1965, and ended five days later at the state capitol in Montgomery, was a turning point not only for the South but for the entire country.

"The Selma-to-Montgomery march had a profound impact on the psyche of all Americans," he said, adding that white students from the

North like us had played a crucial role in ensuring its success. "It was like Gandhi's march to the sea. It transformed American politics."

Those of us who ventured South were called "outside agitators"—a catchy phase that was meant to dishonor us and our cause but that also accurately described what we were up to. Yes, we were agitators. Agitators for justice. "You are here to cause trouble," Dallas County Sheriff Jim Clark told us. And we agreed. "You don't live here," he said. "You are [outside] agitators, and that's the lowest form of humanity."

Not surprisingly, James Farmer, executive secretary of the Congress of Racial Equality (CORE), disagreed, saying we were not outsiders, "because we're Americans." But it was Martin Luther King Jr. who put it best. "Injustice anywhere is a threat to justice everywhere," he wrote in his "Letter from Birmingham Jail" in April 1963. "Anyone who lives inside the United States can never be considered an outsider anywhere within its bounds."

It was, to be sure, a frightening time. President John F. Kennedy had been assassinated. Four young black girls had been killed in a Ku Klux Klan bombing at the Sixteenth Street Baptist Church in Birmingham, Alabama. Three civil rights workers in their early twenties—Michael Schwerner, Andrew Goodman, and James Chaney—had been murdered by the KKK in Mississippi. And the homes and churches of African Americans throughout the South were being attacked and burned on a daily basis.

A young black protestor, Jimmie Lee Jackson, had also been killed by an Alabama state trooper in Marion, just west of Selma, in February 1965. And a white Unitarian minister from Boston, James Reeb, had been beaten to death by four Klansmen outside a restaurant in Selma on March 9, 1965—less than two weeks before the Selma-to-Montgomery would begin.

A joke circulating among civil rights workers at the time had a would-be activist from the North kneeling and praying to God, "Please, Lord, send me a sign that you'll go with me to Mississippi." After a long pause, a deep voice answered, "OK. But I'll only go as far as Memphis."

But it was also a hopeful time. After the Selma-to-Montgomery march, President Johnson signed into law (on August 6, 1965) the landmark Voting Rights Act of 1965, which forbade once and for all the discriminatory voter registration policies and practices that had disenfranchised millions of African Americans. Most historians agree that Johnson and the Congress would not have acted so quickly—or perhaps at all—had it not been for Selma.

This, then, is the story of a small group of college students from the North who, in the spring of 1965, headed South to march for the right of all Americans to vote, and of a small college in the faraway depths of central Wisconsin caught in the crosshairs of a social revolution. It is also the story of some courageous religious leaders and laymen, including Rev. Thompson, who spent the long, heated spring of 1965—and the rest of their lives—making a difference.

CHAPTER 1

The Telegram

Late in the afternoon of March 7, 1965, Andrew Young picked up the phone in Selma, Alabama, and called the Reverend Martin Luther King Jr. to tell him the news.

Young told his longtime friend and mentor, who was in Atlanta that Sunday morning preaching at Ebenezer Baptist Church, that something terrible had just happened.

SNCC Chairman John Lewis and Hosea Williams, an aide to King in the Southern Christian Leadership Conference (SCLC), had been leading about six hundred protesters across Selma's Edmund Pettus Bridge in what was supposed to have been the first leg of a voting rights march to Montgomery, fifty-four miles away, when they were beaten badly by Alabama state troopers and sheriff's deputies hurling tear gas canisters and wielding billy clubs.

Dozens had been injured in the melee, including Lewis, who had suffered a fractured skull. "I'm going to die here," Lewis later recalled, saying his head was bleeding badly and exploding with pain.[1]

Several women, including fifty-three-year-old Amelia Boynton, also lay bloody on the pavement at the foot of the bridge. "As I stepped aside from a trooper's club," she remembered, "I felt a blow on my arm… Another blow by a trooper, as I was gasping for breath, knocked me to the ground and there I lay, unconscious…"[2]

King, of course, was horrified on hearing the news, and it even made him question the wisdom of continuing his strategy of nonviolent protest in Selma and the surrounding communities. But in the end he decided that the planned march from Selma to Montgomery would have to proceed, despite growing fears that further violence would follow. It was too important to be abandoned now, he said.

That evening, as Lewis, Boynton, and dozens of others were being treated for their injuries at the Brown Chapel AME Church in Selma and at the city's largest black health-care facility, Good Samaritan Hospital, images from what had transpired at the foot of the Edmund Pettus Bridge earlier that day were being broadcast across the country by ABC News, which broke into its Sunday night telecast—the television premiere of Stanley Kramer's *Judgment at Nuremberg*—to air the shocking footage.

Forty-eight million viewers watched in horror at the attacks being carried out by Alabama law enforcement officials against defenseless fellow Americans. At one point, the voice of Dallas County Sheriff Jim Clark could be heard yelling, "Get those goddamned niggers!"[3]

Lewis later said that people could not believe what they were seeing. "Women and children being attacked by men on horseback. It was impossible to believe."[4]

But the local newspaper—the *Selma Times-Journal*—played down the the news, saying that the protestors had not dispersed when ordered to do so and were therefore "routed" by the authorities. Several marchers, according to the paper, were "knocked down or fell during the scramble with officers." A brief outbreak of "missile throwing by Negroes," it said, was countered by law officers who drove them back to Brown Chapel. This, it said, was followed by a quick "mop-up operation" that cleared the streets of the city, noting that thirty minutes after the marchers' "encounter" with the state troopers, "a Negro would not be seen walking the streets."[5]

The "mop-up operation" had been merciless. More than a hundred state troopers and sheriff's deputies had chased the marchers over the high-arching steel bridge and for a mile or so back to Selma, attacking with a vengeance those who were left behind. Posse men beat people in front of Brown Chapel and hurled teargas to disperse the crowd.

Among those who observed the attacks and offered aid to the wounded was the Reverend John B. Morris, cofounder of the Episcopal Society for Cultural and Racial Unity (ESCRU) and a leader in the effort to integrate the local Episcopal church.

Morris, who was white, had been on the same flight from Atlanta to Montgomery with Andrew Young earlier in the day, and they had shared a ride to Selma.[6]

It was not the first time that Morris had been involved in the civil rights struggle. The thirty-five-year-old Episcopal priest had been active in the movement since the 1950s and had organized a "Prayer Pilgrimage" in 1961, in which fifteen black and white clergy were arrested and jailed in Jackson, Mississippi, after attempting to eat at a bus station lunch counter. He had also participated in countless other civil rights protests, and under his leadership, ESCRU had organized groups of clergy from around the country to participate in the March on Washington in 1963, where King had delivered his "I Have a Dream" speech.

Now, in March 1965, Morris was in Selma at the epicenter of the movement, where, after aiding injured protesters from the Edmund Pettus Bridge confrontation, he was among those, including Young, who spoke with King in Atlanta by telephone to discuss how the movement should respond to the "Bloody Sunday" attack.

Morris and Young convinced King to issue a call to prominent religious leaders in the North who were known to be sympathetic to the civil rights cause to come to Selma and join him on a voting rights march to the Alabama state capitol in Montgomery. In this way, Morris said, the United States "representatively through its clergy, could bear some of the burden Selma residents had suffered [on Bloody Sunday]."[7]

Within hours, several hundred telegrams signed by King were being sent from SCLC headquarters on Auburn Avenue in Atlanta to every religious leader whose address the organization's program director, Randolph T. Blackwell, could find.[8]

"In the vicious maltreatment of defenseless citizens of Selma," the telegram read, "where old women and young children were gassed and clubbed at random, we have witnessed an eruption of the disease of racism which seeks to destroy all America. No American is without responsibility...I call therefore, on clergy of all faiths to join me in Selma for a ministers march to Montgomery..."

For his part, Morris spent hours on the phone urging his fellow clergymen to come to Selma, and the National Council of Churches' Commission on Religion and Race in New York City issued an appeal of its own, asking pastors and lay leaders from around the country to respond to King's call to action.[9]

Over the next few days, thousands of clergy and other activists from around the country began to descend on Selma to show their solidarity with the movement, including more than five hundred Episcopalians. About 10 percent of all the Episcopal clergy in the country, in fact, including then-presiding Bishop John E. Hines, eventually joined the entourage—over the strong objections of the bishop of the Alabama diocese, Charles C. J. Carpenter, who called the Selma protest "a foolish business and sad waste of time." He urged his fellow Episcopalians to go home. But they did not.[10]

Students at colleges and universities throughout the North were also moved to act.

A twenty-three-year-old student at Chicago Theological Seminary named Jesse L. Jackson, for instance, jumped onto a table in the school cafeteria on Monday, March 8, and shouted, "Pack your bags." Soon, he and about twenty other students and five professors—most of them white—were piling into several cars and heading south, caravan-style, to Selma some 750 miles away.[11]

Also on the move were eleven students from the Episcopal Theological School in Cambridge, Massachusetts, including Jonathan Myrick Daniels, whose twenty-sixth birthday was just two weeks away. He and the other leaders of the student government—after learning, also on March 8, of King's call to come to Selma—had endorsed their participation in the initiative, and $600 was raised to finance their trip.[12]

That evening, at Boston's Logan Field, the ETS students boarded a flight to Atlanta, arriving exhausted but in good spirits in the middle of the night. Anxious and fearful, they spent the rest of the night at SCLC headquarters. Those who were able to sleep at all found comfort in sofas or chairs or on the floor, some in King's own office.

The next day, the group boarded a bus for the five-hour ride to Selma, buoyed by the sights and sounds of movement veterans singing protest songs. But soon their mood turned serious, when the driver of the bus refused to take them beyond Birmingham, saying he feared an attack by white segregationists. A new driver was dispatched, and the bus continued on to Selma.[13]

By now, King had also arrived in Selma, telling an audience of about a thousand, including Daniels, at Brown Chapel late on March 8 that the suffering caused by beatings and the bloodshed at the Edmund Pettus Bridge the previous day had not been in vain. "We must let them know that if they beat one Negro they are going to beat a hundred," he said, "and if they beat a hundred, then they are going to have to beat a thousand."[14]

Following his speech, which ended at around 10:30 p.m., King met with several of his aides, including Andrew Young and Hosea Williams, at the home of Selma's only black dentist, Dr. Sullivan Jackson, to discuss what to do next. Their decision—taken in the early morning hours of March 9—was to proceed with the march to Montgomery later that day, despite an earlier threat by US District Judge Frank M. Johnson Jr. to prohibit the march pending a hearing on the matter.

Daniels and his fellow seminarians, meanwhile, were escorted from Brown Chapel to the George Washington Carver housing project across the street, where they were given a place to sleep.

The next morning, Daniels awoke to find buses, taxis, and rental cars disgorging newcomers to the African American neighborhood surrounding Brown Chapel. An estimated 800 people had arrived from twenty-two states, and the number of demonstrators who were gathering to participate in the expected march over the Edmund Pettus Bridge had grown to 2,000 to 2,500—more than half of them white, including some 450 clergy who had heard King's nationwide appeal to join him in Selma.[15]

Included among the clergy was the Reverend James Reeb, a thirty-eight-year-old Unitarian minister from Boston, who like millions of his countrymen had seen the footage on television the evening of March 7—"Bloody Sunday"—showing black demonstrators being clubbed and teargassed by white law enforcement officials.

"I want to go to Selma," Reeb told his wife, Marie, the next day after receiving a call from the regional office of the Unitarian Universalist Association, whose head office had just received a telegram from King seeking volunteers for the trip to Selma. But his wife was opposed.

"I don't want you to go," she told her husband, pointing to the obvious danger involved. "There are others to go. You belong here." But Reeb insisted. "No," he replied. "I belong there. It's the kind of fight I believe in. I want to be part of it."

That evening, after saying good-bye to his four children, he left for the airport for an 11:00 p.m. charter flight to Atlanta—the same plane that Jonathan Daniels and his fellow seminarians would be on. "I'll be back soon," Reeb told his wife, who dropped him off at the entrance to the airport terminal. "Take care," she responded. "We will be waiting for you."[16]

Like Daniels, Reeb arrived in Selma on Tuesday, March 9, around midmorning. He left his suitcase at Brown Chapel and joined the others—black and white clergymen, SNCC workers, SLCC staff members, and local black townspeople—who were gathering to march later in the day.

Shortly after noon, King emerged from Brown Chapel to address the crowd.

"I say to you this afternoon," he said, "that I would rather die on the highways of Alabama than make a butchery of my conscience." At 2:17 p.m., according to FBI observers, he stepped off, leading the protesters toward the bridge and ignoring an order to desist issued by a US marshal on behalf of Judge Johnson.[17]

But just over the bridge, on US Highway 80 leading to Montgomery, the demonstrators were met by a contingent of state troopers—this time numbering about five hundred—who ordered them to halt. Sensing the possibility of another violent confrontation and not wanting to alienate the federal authorities, particularly since he had not yet received assurances from President Johnson that federal troops would be dispatched to protect the demonstrators, King instructed the marchers to return to Brown Chapel.

Inside the church, King defended his decision to abandon the march. But some SNCC organizers said they had lost faith in his leadership, telling the marchers they should have challenged the state troopers on the other side of the Edmund Pettus Bridge and not turned back.

"Why was there violence on Sunday and none on Tuesday?" SNCC Executive Director James Forman asked the crowd from the pulpit of Brown Chapel. "You know the answer. They don't beat white people. It's Negroes they beat and kill."

One African American resident of Selma, however, responded to Forman by saying that, yes, he was right but then added that the reason "they didn't beat us today [was] because the world was here with us. That's what we want. Don't let these white people feel that we don't appreciate their coming."[18]

That evening, while most of the Episcopal seminarians, except Daniels, were making their way to the airport to return to Boston, Reeb and several other Unitarians headed out for dinner. The place they chose, on the advice of Diane Nash at SCLC headquarters just around the corner from Brown Chapel, was Walker's Cafe, known by locals as Eddie's and frequented exclusively by blacks.

At around 7:30 p.m., after they had finished eating, Reeb's dinner companions—Orloff Miller, also from Boston, and Clark Olsen, from Berkeley, California—stepped outside while Reeb phoned his wife back in Boston to tell her he was staying in Selma another day.

Then, the three ministers started walking in the dark back to Brown Chapel—Olsen on the inside, Miller in the middle, and Reeb closest to the curb. They had only taken a step or two, however, when they noticed four white men across the street coming toward them. "Hey, niggers," one said. "Hey, you niggers." Reeb and Miller did not look back, but Olsen did, just as one of the men was raising a large club or pipe and striking Reeb hard and squarely on the left temple, causing him to stagger and fall to the pavement.

It was over in less than a minute, and the attackers fled into the night after also having beaten Miller and Olsen. "Now you know what it is like to be a real nigger," one of them was heard to say.[19]

Soon, Reeb's speech became increasingly incoherent, and he complained of a severe headache. Back at the SCLC office, an ambulance was called, which took him to Burwell Infirmary, where Dr. William Dinkins—one of only two black physicians in the Selma area—knew at once that there was something seriously wrong. Soon, Reeb fell into a coma and was transferred to University Hospital in Birmingham for the care he required.

The next day the hospital released a statement saying that Reeb's condition was "extremely critical and the prognosis is poor." It said he had sustained multiple skull fractures, and a large blood clot had formed on the left side of the brain.[20]

Later that day hundreds of local people and clergy from around the country, including Jonathan Daniels, set off from Brown Chapel to march several blocks to the Dallas County Courthouse to protest the assault on Reeb. After only a couple of blocks, however, the marchers were stopped by Selma's public safety director, Wilson Baker, and Mayor Joe T. Smitherman, who told them they were banning all marches.

"We are going to stop any demonstrations," Baker told the protesters. "It is too risky under the present circumstances."[21]

This, in turn, led to a standoff on Sylvan Street in front of Brown Chapel between the demonstrators and law enforcement officials that would last for several days—even as Baker was announcing that three of the four men charged in the assault on Reeb had been arrested.

On Thursday, March 11, at around 7:30 p.m., with the three men and a fourth now arrested but already released from jail, Baker showed up at a vigil being held on Sylvan Street to break the news that Reeb had died. He pledged to rearrest the men on murder charges, which he did— only to see them released again later in the week.[22]

Newspapers across the country took note of Reeb's death in their Friday editions, as well as of the growing outrage among the nation's clergy at the events in Selma.

Mass demonstrations in support of the Selma protestors were held in cities across the country, including Washington, DC, where a group of national religious leaders organized protests in front of the White House in an effort to persuade President Johnson to send troops to Selma to protect the marchers.

On Friday morning, according to the Right Reverend Paul Moore Jr., the Episcopal suffragan bishop of Washington, DC, President Johnson acceded to "pressure and the importunities of some of his staff" and agreed to meet with him and about a dozen other leaders of the protests.

"We tried to convey the frustration of the civil rights people and of black America at the apparent lack of sympathy on the part of the White House," Moore wrote, "and to build a case for federal troops to protect the Selma march."

Moore said that the president told them that when the pressure was on him, "like from all of you, I feel like a mule in a hailstorm. I put my head down, hunch up, and let it rain." He said he was deeply sympathetic to the plight of the "Negras."[23]

The next day, after meeting with Alabama Governor George C. Wallace—and as more than a thousand civil rights protesters picketed outside the White House—Johnson met with reporters in the Rose Garden, saying that the events of "Bloody Sunday" in Selma "cannot and will not be repeated." He said that the protests in Selma were against a "deep and very unjust flaw in American democracy itself."

"Ninety-five years ago our Constitution was amended to require that no American can be denied the right to vote because of race or color," Johnson said. "Almost a century later, many Americans are kept from voting simply because they are Negroes."

He said that, therefore, he would soon be sending to Congress legislation that would become known as the Voting Rights Act of 1965. But he did not commit to calling up the National Guard or to sending troops to Alabama, saying only that he was ready to do so if he concluded they were necessary.

"What happened in Selma was an American tragedy," he said. "The blows that were received, the blood that was shed, the life of the good man [Reeb] that was lost, must strengthen the determination of each of us to bring full and equal and exact justice to all of our people."[24]

The standoff between demonstrators and the police on Sylvan Street outside of Brown Chapel in Selma, meanwhile, continued. On Sunday, March 14, the developments in Selma received widespread coverage in newspapers nationwide, and vigils and marches supporting the protesters were held in major cities including New York, Philadelphia, Boston, Cincinnati, Louisville, Toledo, Milwaukee, Los Angeles, and St. Louis, as well as some smaller cities and towns.[25]

A front-page letter signed by Mayor Smitherman and Dallas County Sheriff Jim Clark also appeared in the *Selma Times-Journal* on Sunday asking the people of Selma—"both white and Negro"—to give them their support and prayers as they continued to deal with what they said had become a serious situation.

"For reasons known only to themselves," the two men wrote, "outside racial agitators have chosen to make Selma what they call a 'focal point' in their national drive to raise money, gain political power and to pressure the president of the United States and the Congress of the United States into enacting new and stronger civil rights laws."

Mass demonstrations, meanwhile, continued outside the White House on Monday, while inside the executive mansion a team of speechwriters that had worked through the night revised and tweaked a draft of an address focusing on civil rights that President Johnson was scheduled to deliver at a joint session of Congress that night.

In Selma, plans were being made for a memorial service for Rev. Reeb that afternoon. Dignitaries gathered to pay tribute to him, including presiding Bishop Hines of the Episcopal Church; Walter Reuther, president of the United Auto Workers; and Greek Orthodox Archbishop Iakovos.

The service—presided over by King, who had arrived in Selma from a weekend of speeches in Chicago—was held at Brown Chapel, which was filled with many prominent clergy from around the nation.

King told the audience that Reeb's crime was that he "dared to live his faith." He also spoke dismissively of indifferent religious leaders who "kept silent behind the safety of stained glass windows," and he criticized the federal government for its "timidity" in dealing with the crisis in Selma.

After the service, which Coretta Scott King called "perhaps the greatest and most inspiring ecumenical service ever held,"[26] some 3,500 people, including King, marched to the courthouse for a brief ceremony honoring Reeb and other civil rights martyrs.[27]

That evening, President Johnson went before Congress to say in a nationally televised address that what was happening in Selma was part of a larger movement "which reaches into every section and state of America. It is the effort of American Negroes to secure for themselves the full blessings of American life."

"Their cause must be our cause, too," Johnson said. "Because it is not just Negroes, but really all of us, who must overcome the crippling legacy of bigotry and injustice. And we shall overcome!"

Watching the speech on television at the home of local Selma black dentist, Dr. Sullivan Jackson, were several leaders of the civil rights movement, including King and John Lewis, who was still recovering from the beating he had received at the hands of Alabama state troopers on "Bloody Sunday" a week earlier.

"Along with seventy million other Americans who watched the broadcast that evening," Lewis later recalled, "we listened to Lyndon Johnson make what many others and I consider not only his finest speech of his career, but probably the strongest speech any American president has ever made on the subject of civil rights...His were the words of a statesman and more; they were the words of a poet."

Lewis said he thinks that King must have agreed, noting that he had wiped away a tear when Johnson said, "We shall overcome!"[28]

The next day, US District Judge Frank M. Johnson Jr. ruled that the Selma-to-Montgomery march could proceed, arguing on the basis of an elaborate plan for the fifty-four-mile march written by James M. Nabrit III and his colleagues at the NAACP Legal Defense and Educational Fund that the right to petition the government for the redress of grievances extends to "large groups," and that these rights may be exercised by marching, "even along public highways."

Johnson's ruling thus cleared the way for the march to begin again—this time on March 21. And now it would take place under the protection of the federal government.

CHAPTER 2

"Good-Natured Louts"

As a young college student, listening to President Johnson's speech, I was reminded of how shocked, saddened, and angered I had been when I had first learned earlier in the month of what was happening in and around Selma.

I remember thinking it would be irresponsible of us, even a thousand miles away at Ripon College, a small, mainly all-white liberal arts college in central Wisconsin, not to do something. But what?

Traveling to Selma seemed at first to be unrealistic. We had no money. We had classes to attend and papers to write. And the message being sent by local Alabama law enforcement officials to northerners like us was not encouraging. "You'll march," Dallas County Sheriff Jim Clark said one day, "over my dead body." I remember taking him seriously and thinking that, yes, I was too young to die.

I had decided to attend Ripon College because it was relatively close to home, which was Crystal Lake, Illinois, about 120 miles to the south, yet it was also far enough away to discourage inquiring parents from too many visits.

The city of Ripon and the college campus were also a lot like Crystal Lake: white, mainly Christian, and without any obvious complications.

My best friends in high school were Mike, Lee, Kevin, and Dick. Lee told us one day he wanted to be a millionaire by the time he was thirty. We thought that was a great idea. With Lee in charge, we were on our way—headed for success and doing all the right things to get there. We didn't study much, we played sports and drank beer and smoked cigarettes when we could get away with it, and we went to church on Sunday.

While Rosa Parks was fighting for a seat on the bus, we were preparing to run the company that *owned* that bus.

At Ripon, my friends were Jack, Bill, and David...and a disheveled brainy guy named Dick Grimsrud, from Wauwatosa, Wisconsin, who never said he wanted to be a millionaire—or at least not that I can remember. He thought the world had problems, beginning with Selma, and he wanted to fix them. I also thought that was a great idea.

Over time, I would also cross paths with, and admire for a lifetime, the college chaplain, the Reverend Herman Jerome "Jerry" Thompson, who had clearly missed the millionaire train. Like Dick, he was interested in other things.

Born in Baldwin, Wisconsin, in 1923, Thompson had graduated valedictorian of his Cameron (Wisconsin) High School class in 1941. He attended St. Olaf College in Northfield, Minnesota, before transferring to the University of Wisconsin where he excelled at baseball and football and graduated summa cum laude. He went on to coach a string of successful football and track teams at high schools and colleges across the Midwest.

But in his late thirties—with a wife and four children—he decided to pursue a divinity degree, which he obtained in 1961 from Luther Theological Seminary in St. Paul, Minnesota. The next year, as an ordained Lutheran minister, he established the department of religion at Ripon College, where he served as professor of religion until he retired in 1985. He was also commissioner of the Midwest Collegiate Athletic Conference and chairman of the Fond du Lac County (Wisconsin) Democratic Party. And in his later years as a tennis fanatic, he was ranked first in Wisconsin, second in the Midwest, and nineteenth in the nation among sixty-five-year-olds and older.

For his part, the president of the college, Fred O. Pinkham. had set as a priority pushing through a much-needed face-lift of the campus. During his term in office (1955–1965), he oversaw the construction of new dormitories, a state-of-the-art science building, and several other facilities, which led to a near-doubling in student enrollment, to 822, and an increase in the school's operating budget from $814,000 to $2.2 million.

"Bricks and mortars, endowments and facilities do not alone give meaning to Ripon," he said, "but they are the things that make Ripon possible."

The student body, however, remained decidedly unchanged—concerned about the things that some said had concerned students since the school's founding a hundred-plus years earlier.

George F. Kennan, the American diplomat, political scientist, and historian, whose father attended the school, visited the campus in February 1965 (a month before we left for Selma) to deliver a lecture. He later called our young student faces "open, pleasant ones, but with curiously little written on them at all."

Kennan was perhaps best known as the author of the "Long Telegram" and the subsequent article "The Sources of Soviet Conduct," which set out the strategic vision that would define US policy toward the Soviet Union until its collapse in 1991.

Now, in early 1965 and a week shy of his sixty-first birthday, he was being met at the train station in Columbus, Wisconsin, by members of the Ripon College History Department. From there, he was driven forty or fifty miles to Ripon "over wide straight roads, past frozen, snow-covered fields and prosperous dairy farms with beautiful red barns and less beautiful houses done in the dirty yellow brick of the region...My companions were solemn, correct, and amiable, but a bit intimidated, I suspected, and guarded."

His impressions of the students at Ripon were mixed. The "girls," he said, were more mature than the "men" and superior to them, too, "socially and in style: more cosmopolitan, less provincial, more part of the age, in general more like modern women in Vienna or Milan or wherever else you like than the men of similar age in those places."

He said that Ripon's female students clearly took a larger view than the men of the "competitive sphere in which they considered their lives to evolve—the reflection of an awareness, perhaps, of the relative uniformity in women's problems everywhere."

The Ripon men, however, were "good-natured louts, immersed in their world of records and athletics and fraternities and summer jobs, mildly curious about the great wide world beyond, but less closely keyed to it than the women. It is the woman who is truly international."

Kennan said that he would learn later that his visit to the Ripon had been extremely controversial. His invitation, he said, had come from the History Department, which was chaired by John F. Glaser, and not from the college, which meant that President Pinkham was nowhere to be seen during his visit to the campus.

"I [was] too liberal, if not worse," Kennan wrote, noting the conservative "political atmosphere" of that part of Wisconsin, which he called Republican "Senator [Joseph] McCarthy's state."

By all accounts, Kennan, who was born in Milwaukee, was a Midwesterner at heart (even though he would leave the region for good in 1921, at seventeen years old, to attend Princeton University and never to return to live). His enduring fondness for and understanding of the Midwest was clear in his writings throughout his life.

Recalling his visit to Ripon in 1965, for instance, he captured the uniqueness of the region in his 1989 memoir *Sketches from a Life*, in which he described Wisconsin's "strange, still flatness" as being "like no other flatness, subdued and yet exciting, as though filled with deep unspoken implications…I knew I was close to home."

Kennan said that in the Midwest, a bank of clouds appearing on the horizon could create the illusion of a range of low mountains. "What, one wondered, would life and people have been like had there been such a mountain range there?" he asked. "Life, presumably, would have been more varied, more violent, more interesting; but the massive inert power of the midwestern tradition, with all its virtues and all its weaknesses, sufficient to constitute the spiritual heart of a nation, would not have survived."

He recalled that the face of Ripon was overwhelmingly that of a small New England town, with its wide streets lined with tall trees, spacious lawns, and quiet, well-worn wooden houses. But the houses, he said, were uninspiring, noting that "like so many other Victorians," the builders had prided themselves on the quality of their workmanship and material rather than on creating a thing of beauty.

The old sandstone buildings that dominated the Ripon College campus, moreover, which were "already in existence when my father came to the place ninety-five years ago," were "severe and without architectural ambition, presiding stubbornly, self-assertively, without apology or compromise, over their changed and changing environment."

On the evening of February 11, 1965, as a blizzard began to blow across the wide Wisconsin farm fields, Kennan delivered a lecture to several hundred students (including this writer) and faculty in the school's "bare-boned gymnasium, with its shiny floors, its overhanging basketball boards, and its faint smell of sweaty tennis shoes." Not surprisingly, given his years as a diplomat, he spoke about international affairs and, in particular, the tendency of the United States to make "moral crusades" out of its foreign involvements.

"It is simply not in character for such a country as ours," he told the audience of several hundred, "to try...to produce great changes in the lives of other people, to bring economic development and prosperity to everyone, and to assure to everyone complete peace and security under law."[29]

As Kennan spoke at Ripon, the voting rights campaign that had been launched in Selma by Martin Luther King Jr. at the beginning of the year was now in full swing. On February 1, King was arrested and imprisoned after leading a mass-protest march down Sylvan Street, which focused national attention on his campaign. A front-page article in *The New York Times* the next day appeared under the headline, "Dr. King and 770 Others Seized in Alabama Protest."

As the month wore on, the protests continued—and accelerated—in Selma, the county seat of Dallas County, and in other cities including nearby Marion, the county seat of Perry County.

A seven-page "special report" prepared by the SNCC office in Atlanta, dated February 4, said that plans were also being made to expand its operations to other "Black Belt" counties in Alabama. It said that African Americans made up 57 percent of the Dallas County population, yet only 0.9 percent were registered to vote. Adjoining Wilcox County was 78 percent African American, but no one had been registered. Similar statistics could be found throughout the state.

On February 18, the King-led protests in Selma and surrounding towns that had begun at the beginning of the year came to a head when Alabama state troopers joined local police in Marion to break up an evening march. In the ensuing melee, a twenty-six-year-old pulpwood worker and deacon at St. James Baptist Church named Jimmie Lee Jackson was shot twice in the stomach by one state trooper. He died eight days later in a Selma hospital, which prompted a call by one of King's top advisers and strategists, James Bevel, to call for organizing a march from Selma to Montgomery to petition Governor Wallace to ensure the right of African Americans to vote.

"Be prepared to walk to Montgomery!" Bevel told a mass meeting at Brown Chapel in Selma on February 26. "Be prepared to sleep on the highway!"[30] A few days later, King approved the idea, saying that the march would begin on Sunday, March 7—the day that would be later known as "Bloody Sunday."

It was against this backdrop that some students at Ripon College would look south to what was happening in Selma a thousand miles away. Some said it had nothing to do with them; others thought it did.

Dick Grimsrud and I, along with several other students, discussed the issue and decided to approach Chaplain Thompson, who, we knew, would be sympathetic to initiating some sort of Ripon-sponsored show of support for the civil rights protests in Alabama.

Thompson had already been active in the civil rights movement by, for example, fostering cooperation between students at Ripon and their African American counterparts in the South. In the spring of 1964, he coordinated an exchange program with Tougaloo College, a historically black school of about nine hundred students outside Jackson, Mississippi. Its president was the white civil rights activist and former chaplain at Beloit College in Beloit, Wisconsin, the Reverend Dr. Adam D. Beittel.

The student body at Tougaloo, in fact, had been protesting racial discrimination in Jackson beginning in the 1950s, well before the Thompson-sponsored exchange program took place. Many students had been arrested and jailed for leading a boycott of restaurants that did not serve African Americans and for attempting to attend segregated churches and concerts in and around Jackson, with Beittel frequently raising the money to bail them out of jail.

But by September 1964, the powers-that-be in Mississippi had had enough. The Mississippi State Sovereignty Commission—established by the state legislature in 1956 to defend the state against "encroachment" from the federal government, particularly over civil rights—persuaded Tougaloo's Board of Trustees to dismiss Beittel as college president.

While president, he had hosted a series of exchange programs with several northern schools beginning in 1960, including one with Ripon College, in which I and several other students participated.

For us, of course, the programs were eye-openers, as they were for the students from Tougaloo who had never been out of the South. We were shocked to see first-hand the racial segregation that we had only read about in newspapers being played out in the daily lives of our southern contemporaries. "Water out of a fountain labeled 'colored,'" recalled fellow Ripon student Jim Hess, "tasted just as good as 'white' water to me."

Police brutality—long a mainstay of life for African Americans in the South—was also part of the experience. Walking on a street in downtown Jackson one day, Dick Grimsrud and two other students—Carla Mettling from Lawrence University in Appleton, Wisconsin, and an African

American student from Tougaloo named Kenneth Hayes—were arrested for jaywalking and taken to the police station, where the situation quickly escalated. Mettling and Hayes were hustled upstairs, but Grimsrud was kept behind with the arresting officer. Later, on an elevator, the officer asked Grimsrud a question and slapped him for not saying "sir" when he responded. Then, he kicked and beat the twenty-year-old Grimsrud. Mettling was taken aside by another officer and lectured on "the evils of the Negro." Only later would they be told that the charges against them had been dropped.

William Alexander, a psychology professor at Ripon who accompanied the students to Tougaloo, said on returning to Wisconsin that the exchange-program experience had been valuable because it meant that the Ripon student body could no longer pretend to be "ignorant" of what was happening in the South.

"A clear majority of students at [Ripon College] have become more fully cognizant of the nature of the problem confronting all Americans," he said, "both those in the North and those in the South."

To Alexander, that may have been the case. But to us, few students at Ripon appeared to be moved enough by the tales of what had happened in Tougaloo to think about what they could to do to help ameliorate the situation in Alabama.

Only a dozen or so of us, in fact, were inspired enough to approach Chaplain Thompson for advice, and of that group only four expressed an interest traveling to Selma. Thompson's initial response, however, was circumspect. He said that he was in no position to finance a trip to Selma, although he would certainly contribute some of his own money. We proposed paying for the trip with money allocated by the Student Senate, whose president—truth be told—happened to be a good friend of ours, David Schwarz, a fellow philosophy major (and much smarter).

On Monday, March 15, while violent clashes between demonstrators and the police were taking place near the Alabama state capitol in

Montgomery, Schwarz called a special meeting of the Student Senate at Ripon College.

At nearby Beloit College, the student body, which had already been involved in the civil rights movement through SNCC and the local Civil Rights Interest Group (CRIG), had had little trouble raising nearly $600 to send eight students to Selma. But we knew that seeking financial support from the much more conservative student body at Ripon would be fruitless. Plus, time was not on our side. So we took what we thought would be a more predictable and expeditious route: appealing to the relatively liberal members of the Student Senate for funds. We thought we would need about $400.

At the meeting, which began in the Harwood Memorial Union building at 7:00 p.m. when most students were either studying or heading to the local pub for a beer, Chaplain Thompson rose to our defense, saying that the voting rights legislation that President Johnson was about to send to Congress would not pass unless the pressure that was being generated in Selma was maintained. He said it was important for Ripon College to be represented in Selma.

Also at the meeting that evening was Patrick Hunt, assistant dean of men, who said he had received a call the previous evening from the coordinator of the National Student Association (NSA)—a coalition of college and university student governments—at the University of Wisconsin in Madison, who had asked him if there were students at Ripon who might be interested in joining a delegation from Wisconsin to travel to Selma.

Some members of the Student Senate argued that the money could be better spent elsewhere, like writing a check to the NAACP or inviting a speaker to campus to lecture us on the issue. This caused James R. Bowditch, of the English Department, to blow up, saying that throwing money at the problem would be the worst thing to do. The physical presence of people who care could make all the difference, he said.

In the end, after less than an hour of discussion, the Senate agreed by a vote of thirteen to nine to allocate $400 for the trip to Selma, and in the absence of President Pinkham, the dean of the college, Robert Ashley, assented on behalf of the school administration. Chaplain Thompson was made executor of the funds. He asked those of us who were interested in going to Selma to meet him in his office by 11:00 p.m. to make the necessary arrangements. We agreed that we would leave for Madison (in my Ford Falcon), and eventually Selma, the next day.

CHAPTER 3

Protesting the Protests

The news that the Student Senate had allocated $400 to finance a college-sponsored trip to Selma spread like wildfire through the campus of Ripon College. Students who had earlier been deaf to what was happening down South now found a reason to be outraged.

Leading the protest was Richard Singer, a junior who used his show at the college radio station, WRPN, to urge students to demonstrate their opposition to this alleged misuse of student money at a mass rally the next morning.

At 10:00 a.m. the next day, about 400 angry students—roughly half of the student body—heeded Singer's call and began to converge on Smith Hall, where a meeting involving President Fred O. Pinkham, Dean Robert Ashley, Chaplain Thompson, and Senate President David Schwarz was being held to discuss the Senate's decision. Never before had the school seen such a display of public indignation over an issue.

At the same time, about a thousand miles away in Selma, local law enforcement officials were blocking several voting rights protests. And in Montgomery—in an incident that would make national headlines—police officers on horseback charged a small group of demonstrators that had broken off from a larger contingent of some six hundred mainly young, northern, white protestors and began beating them with canes and nightsticks.

Roy Reed, a reporter for *The New York Times*, wrote in the March 17 edition of the newspaper that one officer in a ten-gallon hat jumped off his horse and "while the horses partly hid him from view, began clubbing the demonstrators. Several still refused to move, and the man's nightstick began falling with great force on their heads." One young man was struck so hard that the sound of the nightstick "carried up and down the block."

Photos of the attack and its victims appeared on the front pages of *The New York Times* and the *Washington Post*.

As the protests in Alabama were unfolding, the student protesters at Ripon College were claiming that the Student Senate had acted inappropriately—i.e., without the full consent of the student body. But more importantly, they were saying that what was happening in Alabama was not school business. As Larry Wilkes, a senior from Connecticut put it, those in the North who cared about civil rights should let southerners handle things as they saw fit. Another senior, Tom Fischer, said that in his view it was "ridiculous" to go to Selma. And members of the Sigma Chi fraternity voted twenty-two to seven to protest the allocation of the funds for our trip to Selma. As Fred Rueger, the president of the Ripon chapter of the fraternity, put it, individuals going to Selma on their own dime was fine; representing the school with school funds was not.

A few students publicly supported what we were planning to do. One was James E. Reed, a sophomore from Seattle, who wrote in the student newspaper, *Ripon College Days*, that those arguing that "we Northerners don't have the right to go meddling in other people's affairs" sounded reasonable on the surface. But that African Americans in the South do not enjoy the same rights as others, he said, is not a local problem but a national issue "because we are one nation and one people."

"The denial of the right to vote to Mississippi Negroes can be a legitimate concern of someone living in Chicago," Reed wrote. "And if this individual is sensitive to the demands of the situation, he has every right—legal and otherwise—to 'meddle in Mississippi affairs.' Perhaps the basic reason that the problem has been so bad for so long is that sensitive people in the North have felt it was none of their business…What is going on on the South today is our problem as well as the South's."

For its part, the school administration said that the Student Senate had acted within its jurisdiction in allocating the funds for our trip. But only one member of the administration—David L. Harris, dean of men—wholeheartedly backed our plan to participate in the ongoing demonstrations down South and the planned voting rights march from Selma to Montgomery, which was set to begin on March 21.

College Dean Robert Ashley said that he had "mixed feelings" about the trip. "I question whether or not any good will be accomplished by the people who go." But he said he respected our "convictions."

Jean Van Hengel, the dean of women, said that the action taken by the Student Senate was legal and proper and "perfectly within their jurisdiction." She said she was upset by the "hasty and emotional demonstration" that was held on campus by students opposing the Senate decision. "I'm not sure it accomplished anything," she said.

Van Hengel also said, however, that while the civil rights protests in the South had played an important role in arousing people's interest and concern and "forcing attention upon the seriousness of the problem, I am not sure whether continuation of the Selma demonstrations is needed."

Dean Harris was less circumspect, saying he applauded the Senate's decision and thought that the student demonstration against it was completely misguided. "Wouldn't you know that once they got off their apathy," he said of the student protesters, "it would be for the wrong reasons?" He said he was ashamed at the "unseemliness" of the protest.

Students traveling to Alabama were members of the Ripon family, Harris said. "We should have been there to shake their hands and see them off," he said. "This way, they left with memories of a screaming crowd, with few people knowing precisely what they were concerned about."

Harris congratulated the Senate for its vote to fund the trip, calling it "courageous." He said that the Senate had finally concerned itself with "something of vital significance to all Americans."

"There is also a great educational opportunity here," he said. "We can go down to Selma and learn something. Do the students really want another jazz concert [funded by the Senate], or do they want a complete, well-rounded education?"

Chaplain Thompson, meanwhile, had his hands full attempting to calm the crowd that confronted him when he emerged from his hour-long meeting with President Pinkham on Tuesday, March 16. He explained that the trip was necessary to show the school's support for civil rights. Then, in a backhanded compliment, he praised the protesters for showing interest in something important "instead of beer and sex."

The crowd, however, showed no signs of dispersing, so we decided to load up the two cars that were taking to Madison. After a brief threat by the protesters to lie down in front of the cars, ten of us—six students and four faculty members—were on our way, arriving in Madison a couple of hours later, where we were quickly herded onto one of several buses headed for Selma.

But on arriving in Chicago, we were informed by the organizers (mainly from SNCC) that the situation in Alabama had become too dangerous for us to proceed, citing the beating of white college students in Montgomery the day before, as well as the ongoing violence and tension in Selma, where a memorial service had just been held for the Reverend James Reeb, the white Unitarian minister from Boston who had been beaten to death by white segregationists.

Disappointed, we were told that the new destination for what had earlier been our Selma-bound bus would be Washington, DC. There we would join protesters at a demonstration outside the White House to demand that President Johnson send federal troops to Alabama to protect the civil rights protesters from the wrath of the state and local law enforcement establishment.

We arrived in the nation's capital, in fact, in the middle of a raging snowstorm—having left Wisconsin supposedly for the warmer South. And quickly, we were ushered to the sidewalk in front of the White House to join twenty to thirty other students wrapped in sleeping bags sitting in the slush against the fence, surrounded by dozens of police and reporters. We were dirty and tired. But most of all, we were angry. We wanted to be in Selma where the real action was.

The protests at the White House were being led by the Reverend Paul Moore Jr., the suffragan Episcopal bishop of Washington, DC, along with other activists. "The thrill of seeing so many citizens, black and white, exerting their power directly to the President was intoxicating," Moore later wrote.[31]

Intoxicating, too, he said, was the meeting he and about a dozen other protest leaders were eventually able to secure with the president. "We took our seats around the Cabinet table," he wrote, "and in a few minutes the President entered...He greeted us courteously...We tried to convey the frustration of the civil rights people and of black America at the apparent lack of sympathy on the part of the White House and to build the case for federal troops to protect the Selma march."

A couple of days later, on March 20, Johnson came through, notifying Governor Wallace that he was mobilizing the Alabama National Guard to protect the planned march from Selma to Montgomery, due to begin the next day.

But we had a problem. We were running out of money. So we did what seemed natural at the time—we called on our representatives on Capitol Hill: Senator William Proxmire (D), who had been elected in a special election in August 1957 following the death of Joseph McCarthy, and Representative John A. Race (D), who was elected in 1964 on the coattails of Lyndon B. Johnson.

Race, whose district included Ripon, sent a letter to President Pinkham at Ripon College after meeting us, saying he admired the students he had met and was confident that Pinkham did as well.

But it was Proxmire who really cleared the way for us to continue to Selma. After meeting with us, he asked one of his aides to accompany us while we solicited contributions from sympathetic members of Congress, and he arranged for us to meet Bishop Moore.

I recall Moore being larger than life (six foot four), greeting us with a bear hug (unusual for the day) and telling us he would "loan" us fifty dollars each for the trip to Selma from his "discretionary fund," which we assumed (correctly, as it turned out) had been set aside for liberal causes.

Moore had grown up a son of privilege—a great-nephew of the Republican senator and political kingmaker from Ohio, Mark Hanna, and a grandson of the founder of Bankers Trust. He graduated from St. Paul's School and Yale University, as did his father before him. But after earning the Navy Cross, a Silver Star, and a Purple Heart in World War II, he devoted the rest of his life to advocating on behalf of the poor and the marginalized members of society, ministering for years in the slums before being named suffragan bishop of Washington, DC, in 1964. Later, he went on to become bishop of New York and, in 1976, to voice his support for the ordination of female priests. He was also a highly vocal and effective opponent of the war in Vietnam. He would die in 2003 at the age of eighty-four.

After meeting Moore, and with two hundred dollars in "loans" from the Episcopal Church and another twenty-five dollars from the Reverend Harris T. Hall of St. Peter's Episcopal Church in Ripon, four of us—Chaplain Thompson, Dick Grimsrud, Noel Carota, and I—rented a car from Hertz and took off for Atlanta. The others who had begun the trip with us returned to Ripon. In Atlanta, we boarded a bus for Birmingham, Alabama—known as "Bombingham" because of the racially motivated bombings by white segregationists who had terrorized the African American residents of the city for years, including on the morning of September 15, 1963, when nineteen sticks of dynamite planted at the Sixteenth Street Baptist Church by four members of the Ku Klux Klan killed four young black girls.

Now, less than two years later, on March 20, 1965, I was concerned for our own lives as we changed buses at the Greyhound bus station in Birmingham. We must have stood out as "outside agitators" with our rolled-up sleeping bags and northern dialects. Four years earlier, several Freedom Riders at this very bus station had been singled out for attack with baseball bats, iron pipes, and bicycle chains by a mob of white racists, aided by the Birmingham police. I remember wanting desperately to board the bus to Selma as quickly as possible.

We arrived in Selma that evening and were welcomed at the West Trinity Baptist Church, where we would spend the night and where the women of the congregation prepared meals for us and our fellow marchers.

From there, Noel Carota telephoned his mother in Massachusetts to say he had arrived in Selma. He told us later that his mother had been one of thirteen conservative activists who had gathered at the Parker House in Boston in 1963 to launch a "Draft Goldwater" campaign.

After "checking in" at the West Trinity Baptist Church, we made our way over to Brown Chapel, several blocks away, where a rally was being held to fire up the crowd for the march to Montgomery the next day. Among the speakers were the Reverend James Bevel, an aide to Martin Luther King Jr. who had proposed the march; Andrew Young; and John Lewis. But it was the comedian Dick Gregory who electrified the crowd by saying that it would be just their luck to discover on arriving in Montgomery "that Wallace is colored."[32]

The organizers of the march, according to John Lewis, had spent several days in a "swirl of activity, much like preparing an army for assault," planning for the march. Thousands of "outsiders" had come to Selma to participate, he said, and thousands of dollars were being spent on everything from food to security. Four tents large enough to sleep hundreds of marchers on stops along US Highway 80 over the next five days were rented at $430 each. Seven hundred air mattresses were purchased. Seven hundred blankets were donated by local schools and churches. And two 2,500-watt generators had been acquired to light the campsites at night.

Walkie-talkies, flashlights, pots, pans—the list seemed endless. A crew of twelve clergymen called the "fish and loaves committee" was charged with transporting food to each campsite each evening. Ten local women cooked meals in church kitchens around Selma. Ten others made sandwiches.

On orders from President Johnson, more than 1,800 armed members of the Alabama National Guard would line the fifty-four-mile route of the march, along with more than one thousand US Army troops, one hundred FBI agents, and one hundred US marshals. Helicopters and light planes would patrol the skies watching for snipers. And federal demolition teams would be assigned to inspect bridges and other potential targets for explosives.[33]

President Johnson told Governor Wallace that he was disappointed at Alabama's failure to carry out its normal law enforcement functions, adding that the federalized National Guard units—reinforced by army regulars—"will help you meet your responsibility."

At a press conference at his ranch in Texas on Saturday, March 20, Johnson said that during the five-day march, "the eyes of the nation will be on Alabama, and the eyes of the world will be on the nation." He said that after the dust had settled, the United States would emerge a stronger, more united country.

But over the weekend of March 20–21, tension remained high in and around Selma, despite the promise of a massive federal presence, with white segregationists continuing to look for ways to disrupt or to blunt the impact of the event.

Former Birmingham Mayor Art Hanes, who in 1962 had closed city parks in violation of a federal order to integrate, announced plans for a reverse march by whites from Montgomery to Selma, which he only canceled after Governor Wallace asked citizens to "stay away from the scenes of tension."

In Selma, a number of residents had asked for permission to stage a counter-demonstration—a request that Mayor Joe T. Smitherman and Dallas County Sheriff Jim Clark eventually turned down.

"We fully understand the motives which have prompted this request," the two officials said in a joint statement, noting that the request had come from "a large number of our friends and fellow white citizens from Alabama and other states…" They said that the "abuses" of the Negro and "transient white demonstrators...have plagued our city for nine weeks." But in the end, they said, "our best course to follow is to try to minimize and curtail all demonstrations, so that our community can continue to operate on as normal a basis as possible...We assure you that as a united community, this, too, 'We Shall Overcome,' so that we may resume our vital task of building a progressive and more prosperous community for all of our citizens."

In Montgomery, meanwhile, about two hundred pro-segregation protestors assembled in front of the Federal Building under the leadership of the Organization for Better Government, carrying signs that read "Outside Clergy, Go Home," "Pious Phonies, Go Home," and "LBJ and MLK, Get Off Our Backs."

One of the leaders of the protest, the Reverend Russell Pate, said that Martin Luther King Jr. and the clergy from other states were making a mockery of religion. "I do not believe in integration," he said, "and I believe I have the Bible to back me up." He blamed the downfall of the Roman Empire on interracial marriage and warned that the same fate could face the United States.

The Methodist bishop of Alabama, the Reverend W. Kenneth Goodson, said that in his view the Selma-to-Montgomery march would do a "great disservice to the cause of human freedom...I counsel all Methodists against participation."

CHAPTER 4

"A Sad Waste of Time"

We awoke in Selma just after dawn on Sunday, March 21, 1965, stiff and aching from a long night on the hard pews of the West Trinity Baptist Church.

After breakfast, Chaplain Thompson, Noel Carota, Dick Grimsrud, and I made our way to Brown Chapel AME Church, where the march was scheduled to begin at 10:00 a.m. in chilly but sunny air. On the way, we learned that a white student from Boston University had been attacked by a local white resident and slashed across the face with a razor blade.

We also learned from *The Selma Times-Journal* that several voting rights demonstrations around the city on Friday had prompted a number of "irate husbands" to leave work to check on their families. Most of the demonstrators, the newspaper said, were "clergymen and beatnik whites."

The newspaper also reported that Robert M. Shelton, the Grand Wizard of the United Klans of America, had announced plans to hold a mass meeting on Sunday in Montgomery to protest the Selma-to-Montgomery march, saying it would be a "peaceful protest."

On our way to Brown Chapel, we passed the First Baptist Church, which was being used as the headquarters of SNCC. Several veteran civil rights workers in bibbed denim overalls were mingling outside with new white recruits from the North, like us.

We would later learn some SNCC leaders, in fact, including its militant executive secretary, James Forman, were threatening to boycott the march over what they believed to be the passivity of Martin Luther King Jr.'s Southern Christian Leadership Conference (SCLC) and the ineffectiveness of such demonstrations. But in the end, after several days of negotiations, it was agreed that individual SNCC members would be allowed to participate in the march but that SNCC as an organization would not.

Later in the day, Dick Grimsrud attempted to engage Forman in conversation. But the civil rights leader rejected his request, making it clear he was not interested in chatting with some white college student from the North.

Over the years, Forman would become increasingly frustrated with what he saw as the gradualist and ineffective approach taken by King and other civil rights leaders in addressing racial injustice. He flirted with the Black Panthers and wrote a book, *The Making of Black Revolutionaries*, in which he devoted an entire chapter to laying out his reasons for dismissing God and other "religious crap." Even in Selma, he did not hide the fact that he had problems with the theory and practice of nonviolence, saying in a fiery speech at Brown Chapel on the evening of March 15, for example, that "if we can't sit at the table [of democracy], let's knock the fuckin' legs off." By January 1966, he had lost all patience with nonviolence—"even as a tactic."[34]

At around 8:00 a.m. we arrived at Brown Chapel, well before the planned start of the march, eager to see King and the other civil rights "celebrities." In a nearby field, Andrew Young was offering last-minute instructions to the march marshals on the importance of remaining nonviolent—an admonition that would have made Forman deeply uncomfortable, had he been there.

"If you're beaten," Young told the marshals, "put your hands over the back of your head. Get to know the people in your unit, so you can tell if somebody's missing or if there's somebody there who shouldn't be there. And listen! If you can't be nonviolent, let me know now."

The crowd waiting for the march to begin was a motley assortment of factory workers, schoolteachers, ministers, nuns, labor leaders, college students, firemen—people from all backgrounds, from all over the United States, black and white, Native Americans and Asian. An estimated three thousand protestors would eventually show up for the beginning of the march.

Among the dignitaries in attendance were Ralph J. Bunche, undersecretary for special political affairs at the United Nations and a Nobel Peace Prize laureate; A. Philip Randolph, the African American labor organizer; Rabbi Abraham Heschel, a leading Jewish theologian and philosopher; James Baldwin, the writer; and Harry Belafonte, the entertainer and civil rights activist.

As for King, he had spent the night at the home of Dr. Sullivan Jackson, a local dentist who, with his wife, Jean, were devout and long-standing supporters of the civil rights movement. His home was next door to the West Trinity Baptist Church, where we had stayed the night. FBI agents would later report that King's entourage arrived at Brown Chapel at 10:58 a.m., almost an hour after the march was scheduled to begin.[35]

It was difficult—even for us only a few yards from the steps of Brown Chapel—to hear the homilies being delivered by the clergy in advance of the march because of the noise of helicopters overhead. But when King began to speak, it was different.

"You will be the people that will light a new chapter in the history books of our nation," he boomed. "Walk together, children. Don't you get weary, and it will lead us to the Promised Land. And Alabama will be a new Alabama, and America will be a new America."

Then, at 12:46 p.m., the crowd began to move slowly down Sylvan Street, with King and Ralph D. Abernathy along with Bunche, Heschel, and Lewis leading the way. A fellow marcher pointed to Walker's Cafe, where the Reverend James Reeb had suffered the devastating blows by several whites on March 9 that would end his life.

At Alabama Avenue, we turned right and saw the first of many local white citizens we would encounter along the route. Here, they lined the street and were silent. But as we turned left onto Broad Street—the city's main thoroughfare and also US Highway 80 to Montgomery—loudspeakers blared "Bye, Bye, Blackbird," and white onlookers began to jeer. Later, a private plane flew overhead dropping hate leaflets on us.

Six abreast, we approached the Edmund Pettus Bridge. It was the third time since "Bloody Sunday," March 7, that voting rights protesters were about to cross the high, arching steel structure over the Alabama River, headed for Montgomery. I remember thinking as we walked at the front of the sea of marchers trailing a mile or more behind that we would all die instantly if some maniac were to dynamite the bridge from below.

The police, meanwhile, had closed off the two eastbound lanes of the four-lane highway, enabling us to proceed safely and smoothly. But the two westbound lanes remained open to traffic, which included a black Volkswagen with "martin luther kink," "walk, coon," and "coonsville, u.s.a." whitewashed on its fenders and doors. Several white children lined the road waving toy guns and chanting "Nigger lover!" and "White nigger!" as loudly as they could.

Another Volkswagen navigating the westbound lanes carried two Episcopal seminarians, Jonathan Myrick Daniels and Judith Upham, who were returning to Selma despite an un-Christian piece of advice from the Episcopal bishop of Alabama, Charles C. J. Carpenter, that all Episcopalians from outside the South should stay away.

"This 'march' is a foolish business and sad waste of time," Carpenter was quoted as saying, "[which reflects] a childish instinct to parade at great cost to our state."

Daniels and Upham, who had been in Selma earlier in the month protesting and working to integrate St. Paul's Episcopal Church, had returned to their studies at the Episcopal Theological School in Cambridge, Massachusetts, for several days. And now, they were returning to Selma to fulfill part of what they saw as their calling to devote their lives to the cause of civil rights. As Daniels put it, "Something had happened to me in Selma which meant I had to come back. I could not stand by in benevolent dispassion any longer without compromising everything I know and love and value. The imperative was too clear, the stakes were too high..."

I do not recall seeing the Volkswagen carrying Daniels and Upham traveling in the opposite direction, toward Selma. But they would later say that they had saluted to the last of the marchers coming down the Edmund Pettus Bridge to the flat land on the Montgomery side, before heading to the George Washington Carver Homes, opposite Brown Chapel, where they would spend the night.

Now, across the bridge, as we passed diners, gas stations, and Craig Field Air Force base, several cars continued to drive by us with signs that were decidedly unwelcoming: "Yankee Trash Go Home," "I Hate Niggers," "Come to Alabama and Be Ruled by King."

Small groups of white onlookers yelled insults and threats, and some waved Confederate flags. One woman stopped her car briefly, exited, stuck out her tongue, climbed back in, slammed the door, and drove off.

Selma Mayor Joseph T. Smitherman told reporters he was "glad to get these people out of town. But I am afraid some of them will come back."

As darkness approached, after walking about seven miles, we turned off US Highway 80 onto a small road leading up to a farm owned by a black man named David Hall, who had agreed to allow the marchers to pitch tents and spend the night. Did he fear retaliation from local whites for doing so? "The Lord," he answered, "will provide."

By dusk, four large canvas tents had been set up for the select few—a total of three hundred—who would be allowed to march the next day, while the rest of us were sent back to Selma.

Those returning to Selma also included SNCC Chairman John Lewis, whose doctors had insisted that after his beating on "Bloody Sunday," he should sleep in a real bed every night during the march and not in a tent out in the cold.

"My head was still bothering me badly enough that I agreed with them," he said later. "I would walk the entire fifty-four-mile route, but I spent each night back in Selma, with a doctor nearby…"[36]

Lewis said, however, that he did not get tired. "You really didn't get weary," he said. "You had to go—it was more than an ordinary march. To me, there was never a march like this one before; there hasn't been one since."[37]

CHAPTER 5

Covering the "Race Beat"

The importance of the national news media in ensuring the success of the voting rights campaign launched by Martin Luther King Jr. in the South cannot be overstated. And no one knew it better than King himself, who often berated reporters for not doing their "duty" to portray racial injustice in the starkest of terms.

"The world doesn't know this happened, because you didn't photograph it," King once told *Life* photographer Flip Schulke when he dropped his camera and began helping several black children being manhandled by Alabama law enforcement officers. "It is so much more important for you to take a picture of us getting beaten up than for you to be another person joining in the fray."[38]

Some reporters, however, like Renata Adler of *The New Yorker*, were unimpressed by what they were witnessing in the march from Selma to Montgomery.

"It was unclear what such a demonstration could hope to achieve," Adler observed. "Few segregationists could be converted by it, the national commitment to civil rights would hardly be increased by it…and for the local citizenry it might have a long and ugly aftermath."

But most reporters who were assigned to the "race beat" understood full well the importance of the march and its potential historical significance.

I was too young at the time to know personally any of the reporters who covered the march, including Paul Montgomery of *The New York Times*, who, at twenty-eight years old, was one of the best. Later, however, he and I would briefly cross paths when we were both posted in Brussels in the 1980s.

Born in Brooklyn, Montgomery was hired by the *Times* as a copy boy in 1959 and soon became a reporter, assigned initially to the metropolitan desk. In early 1965, as the civil rights struggle in the South was heating up, he was sent to Selma.

He was one of the few reporters assigned to cover the "race beat" who, in fact, was not from the South. He did not know how to drive—a fact that the paper's national news editor, Claude Sitton, would learn only after the young reporter had taken up his post in Selma. Tongue in cheek, Sitton wondered whether the metro section editors who had loaned Montgomery to him knew that there were no subways in the South and that you could not hail a taxicab from a cotton field.[39]

Yet Montgomery, along with fellow *Times* reporter Roy Reed, would have little trouble dealing with the situation at hand, walking the entire fifty-four miles from Selma to Montgomery through rain and baking sun and filing elegant and riveting reports from the field over the course of four days and five nights.

"There were civil rights leaders and rabbis, pretty coeds and bearded representatives of the student left, movie stars and infants in strollers," Montgomery wrote in a dispatch filed on the first day of the march, Sunday, March 21. "There were two blind people and a man with one leg. But mostly there were Negroes who believe they have been denied the vote too long."[40]

Less colorful but nonetheless instructive were the daily updates on the march filed by Joseph A. Califano Jr., who reported back to the government agencies in Washington, DC, that had an interest in ensuring the overall safety of the event: the White House, the State Department, the Justice Department, and the Defense Department.

At noon on the second day of the march—Monday, March 22—Califano reported that the marchers had stepped off at 8:06 a.m. in cold weather (twenty-eight degrees). "The marchers were tired, having spent most of the night around the fire to keep warm," he wrote. "There were about 392 people in the column, of which approximately 45 are white… The spectators have been mostly negro."

Califano also reported that a bomb had been found at a school in Birmingham and that a demolition team had been sent to the scene. "There is no further information on this at present."

The incident that Califano referred to was one in a series of planned bombings by segregationists in Birmingham and the surrounding area apparently intended to coincide with the Selma-to-Montgomery march.

According to an AP story in *The Selma Times-Journal*—the local newspaper that reporters from outside Alabama relied on for providing detailed and reliable accounts of civil rights activity in the region—six bombs had been discovered in and around Birmingham in two days.

The story, by AP reporter Jim Purks, said that homemade bombs had been found in the parking lot of an African American funeral home; near the former home of the Reverend A. D. King, the brother of Martin Luther King Jr.; at a Catholic church in an area of the city called "Dynamite Hill" because of past racial bombings; and at Western Olin High School, an African American school in suburban Ensley. All of the bombs, the story said, were successfully disarmed by army demolition teams.

By March 1965, in fact, Purks had become something of an expert on the bombings in Birmingham, having covered initially the most notorious such incident—the dynamiting by the KKK of the Sixteenth Street Baptist Church in 1963.

Walking nearby just after the explosion, Purks hastily scribbled a series of unconnected notes in his reporter's notebook: "[S]everal cars outside twisted and wrecked, windows in 2nd floor broken—Negroes looking…People walking over crumpled glass. Pieces of rock. 'My grandbaby 11 years old—pulled rocks off her'…Clock stopped at 10:25…Patches of blood among the glass—one piece of glass."[41]

It was *The New York Times,* however, that would continue to provide the most extensive coverage of the civil rights movement of any "non-Southern" newspaper.

Sensing the increasing importance of the story to a national audience, the paper hired Roy Reed, formerly of the *Arkansas Gazette,* to cover the voting rights campaign in Selma (launched by Martin Luther King Jr. in early January 1965), along with John Herbers (and later, Paul Montgomery).

Colleagues called Reed unfailingly accurate, deeply reflective, and uncommonly polite. He could write magically, they said. And like a number of other reporters for the *Times* who had preceded him in the South, he spoke "Southern."[42]

On the first day of the Selma-to-Montgomery march, Reed filed a report saying it had already taken on enormous historical significance. "The marchers are well aware," he wrote, "that the armed forces of the United States are poised to protect them and that no matter how peacefully or violently the thing is carried off, it will be long remembered."

On day two of the march, Reed reported that the three-hundred-odd "freedom marchers" had "plodded 16 more miles through the sunny Alabama countryside...before stopping for the night in the heart of Lowndes County—which many Negroes regard as hostile territory."

Reed said that the marchers sang "we are not afraid" as they crossed the Dallas-Lowndes county line at 12:13 p.m. "But Lowndes is lonesome country," he wrote, "and the marchers, if not afraid, are at least a little nervous."

He said that the rolling farmland gave way to marshes and small swamps, and that the marchers had been advised to watch for water moccasins sunning themselves on the road.

"But what the marchers are really watching for," Reed wrote, "are embittered white men, the kind who flew a small plane over the march this morning and threw out leaflets advertising: 'Operation Ban—selective hiring, firing, buying, selling—an unemployed agitator ceases to agitate.'"

Califano, of the Defense Department, wrote in a report filed at 2:00 p.m. that the marchers—arranged in six, fifty-man groups walking three abreast and including thirty-seven whites—had stopped for lunch at the start of the two-lane highway near Benton. He said that John Lewis, who had returned to Selma to spend the night of March 21–22, had rejoined the marchers. "The age of the marchers runs generally between twelve and twenty," Califano reported. "One-third are female."

Leading the procession were Martin Luther King Jr. and his wife, Coretta, along with LeRoy Collins, director of the Community Relations Service, representing President Johnson.

At dusk, King and the rest of the marchers arrived at the day's campsite—an open field next to a grocery store owned by Rosie Steele, a seventy-eight-year-old widow, near the edge of Big Swamp Creek. His feet were in "poor condition," his wife later reported, and he was treated by a doctor.

Before bedding down for the night, however, King was told that a plot to assassinate him had been uncovered. The suspected assailant, according to his wife, was "a man disguised as a minister." But King refused to alter his plans, which called for continuing to march then flying to Cleveland the next day to raise money. "While we maintained unarmed guards," his wife wrote, "we understood the FBI was on hand guarding Martin all the time."[43]

Local law enforcement officials like Lowndes County Sheriff Frank Ryals had little use for King and his followers, calling them "beatniks and screwballs and people like that."

"This march is uncalled for," he said. "It's a lot of expense for nothing. It's disrupting people in their homes and on the highway...We have been getting along fine here. And we will continue to unless they come in here with a whole lot of this unlawful stuff and this provocation."[44]

Not surprisingly, Ryals enjoyed the overwhelming support of the county's white population. But he also won over nationally syndicated columnists Rowland Evans and Robert Novak, who argued that Stokely Carmichael's provocative presence in Lowndes County had made it impossible for Ryals to abandon his "hereditary segregationism."

Evans and Novak wrote that Ryals—"no belly-bumping Southern sheriff, but a soft-spoken farmer criticized by local Klansmen as too soft"—had become "increasingly alienated from the Negro" because of the push for African American voting rights in the county.

Earlier, Evans and Novak had claimed said that Martin Luther King Jr. had relinquished command of the Selma movement demonstrations to John Lewis and James Foreman ("two hothead extremists"), adding that SNCC had been "substantially infiltrated" by "beatnik left-wing revolutionaries, and—worst of all—by Communists."[45]

The local press in Alabama also had a problem with beatniks. A front-page story in the March 22 issue of *The Selma Times-Journal,* for instance, said that the participants in the Selma-to-Montgomery march included priests, nuns, ministers, rabbis, and "beatniks types." Also present, it said, were white women, Negro civil rights leaders, and a Negro pushing his baby in a stroller. "Some were well-dressed," it said, "some wore Levi's."

Some members of the "press" were more sympathetic, including four students at Grinnell College—a small liberal arts school in central Iowa—who were so moved by the events in Selma on "Bloody Sunday" that they decided to drive south immediately and report on what they saw.

One of the students, Henry Wilhelm, later recalled that as staff members of the Grinnell College newspaper *Scarlet & Black*, they had quickly sensed the importance of what was unfolding in Selma. "And two days later," he said, "[we] climbed into my VW bug and drove straight to Selma," arriving twenty hours later.

The stories and pictures they filed to their editor back at Grinnell, John Wolf, were fresh and remarkably insightful, given their age.

"One drives into Selma and encounters a never-never land," wrote Robert Hodierne, another student. "It's kind of an Alfred Hitchcock version of Alice in Wonderland." He said that Selma is an old town with old customs. "The customs are hard to change…"

Hodierne, who later would become an award-winning professional reporter/photographer, argued in a special edition of *Scarlet & Black* dated March 20, 1965, that Selma represented a major turning point in the civil rights movement because, for the first time, it involved religious leaders from across the country.

"In the past, the churches made statements supporting civil rights but had never been active," he wrote.

Hodierne wrote that Selma's public safety director, Wilson Baker, was unique among southern police in that he attempted "impartial and objective law enforcement"—an assessment that may have been too generous given that Wilson had been and remained a proud segregationist throughout his entire life.

"It goes without saying that these [white] people [in Selma] hate Negroes," Hodierne wrote. "Even more they hate the press which exposes them to the world. But even more, they hate the northern college students. The four of us are an unfortunate combination—northern college student pressmen."

Hodierne said that he and Harold Fuson, also a reporter for *Scarlet & Black*, had managed to obtain press credentials "though means which would make a red-neck indignant and probably make Sheriff Clark furious." As for Wilhelm and the fourth student, John F. Phillips—both photographers—they were fearless in going everywhere with their cameras but without press credentials, with everyone simply assuming they were members of the press.

"In the few words I have here," Hodierne wrote, conceding that there were limits to their ability to accurately portray what was happening right in front of them, "I cannot begin to describe the Selma demonstration. It is a situation that will require millions of words and hundreds of pictures. We have lived with demonstrators, police and townspeople, yet I'm not sure any of us could begin to draw a clear picture of it all. You have to come to Selma to know Selma."

CHAPTER 6

The Clergy Heeds the Call

On the third day of the march—Tuesday, March 23—the heavens opened up, flooding the campsite the marchers had used the night before, halfway between Selma and Montgomery. And just after 8:00 a.m., with the rain expected to continue for most of the day, they stepped off in a cold drizzle onto US Highway 80 heading east.

Among those now present for the march were large numbers of Christians, Jews, and others from the religious community who had heeded Martin Luther King Jr.'s call to come to Alabama to support the voting rights campaign.

The Episcopalian contingent was particularly impressive—perhaps reflecting decades of pent-up guilt over the denomination's sad stance on race relations. It included Jonathan Daniels, the young Episcopal seminarian from Boston, who stood guard at the campsite as part of a security force organized by the Reverend Morris V. Samuel Jr., another Episcopalian, from Los Angeles.[46]

Also comprising the contingent were roughly five hundred others, including the Right Reverend John E. Hines, the presiding bishop of the Episcopal Church. It didn't take long for them to turn their attention while in Selma to what they saw as another pressing civil rights issue—beyond voting rights—that needed to be addressed: the longstanding ban on African Americans worshipping at the city's Episcopal church, St. Paul's, located in the relatively prosperous white section of the city.

Daniels and about two dozen other Episcopal seminarians and clergy began their quest for church justice one day by walking from Brown Chapel to St. Paul's to meet the rector, the Reverend T. Frank Matthews, who, in a brief session with them, forcefully defended the parish policy of prohibiting interracial worship—even though doing so directly contravened a resolution adopted by the General Convention of the Episcopal Church several months earlier prohibiting discrimination on the basis of race, color, or ethnic origin.

Matthews told the group that at his church it was up to the ushers to decide whether to admit African Americans. But most of them, he said, would bar any integrated group from entering, and he could do nothing about it if he wanted to keep his job.

For Daniels and the other Episcopalians, the only choice, it seemed, was to challenge the policy by showing up with an interracial group for Sunday worship.

Led by the Reverend John B. Morris, executive secretary of the Episcopal Society for Cultural and Racial Unity (ESCRU), and Malcolm Peabody, president of the ESCRU board of directors, the group was met at the church door by a phalanx of ushers intent on, as Morris joked at the time, "guarding the church from the Church." Only members of the clergy and white lay people would be allowed to enter, the ushers said—a condition that Morris and the others refused to accept. So they kneeled for a moment of prayer and left.

Another attempt at integrating the church came on Saturday, March 20, the day before the start of the Selma-to-Montgomery march. It was led by the Reverend C. Kilmer Myers, the suffragan bishop of Michigan, who had sought permission from the bishop of the Alabama diocese, the Right Reverend Charles C. J. Carpenter, to celebrate Eucharist at St. Paul's with an integrated congregation, arguing that, as a bishop, he had the right to celebrate Eucharist at any Episcopal parish he visited.

But Carpenter refused to order Matthews and the church vestry to honor Myers's request.

Two years earlier—in April 1963—Carpenter had caused a stir by signing, along with seven other religious leaders in Alabama, an open letter to Martin Luther King Jr. calling for an end to the mass demonstrations that were being led by King in Birmingham.

"We recognize the natural impatience of people who feel that their hopes are slow in being realized," the letter, published in the *Birmingham News* on April 12, said. "But we are convinced that these demonstrations are unwise and untimely…[They] have not contributed to the resolution of our local problems." Racial matters, it said, should properly be pursued in the courts. "When rights are consistently denied," it said, "a cause should be pressed in the courts and in negotiations among local leaders, and not in the streets." It said that the demonstrations were being led "in part by outsiders."

In response, while confined to a Birmingham jail for violating a court injunction against street protests, King scribbled on scraps of paper smuggled into his cell what would become perhaps the most important written document of the civil rights era: "Letter from Birmingham Jail."

The letter, typed up later by an aide and published in full by the *Christian Century*, set out the case for pursuing nonviolent civil disobedience as a means of addressing racial injustice and offered a blistering critique of "white moderates," who, he said, "paternalistically" believed that they could set a timetable for another man's freedom.

King said in his twenty-page response dated April 16 that, yes, he was not from Alabama but that he had come to Birmingham "because injustice is here."

"Injustice anywhere is a threat to justice everywhere," he wrote in one of his most widely quoted lines. "We are caught in an inescapable network of mutuality, tied in a single garment of destiny. Whatever affects one directly, affects all indirectly."

Today, those lines appear prominently with thirteen other quotations from King's speeches, sermons, and writings inscribed on a stone wall at the Martin Luther King Jr. Memorial in Washington, DC.

King said he was sorry that Carpenter and the other clergymen, while deploring the demonstrations, had failed to show similar concern for the conditions that had prompted the demonstrations. "It is unfortunate that demonstrations are taking place in Birmingham," he said, "but it is even more unfortunate that the city's white power structure left the Negro community with no alternative."

He said that no gain in the civil rights movement had ever been made without persistent legal and nonviolent pressure from concerned citizens. Freedom, he said, is never voluntarily given by the oppressor; it must be demanded by the oppressed.

King told what he called his "Christian and Jewish brothers" that, moreover, he was extremely disappointed with the behavior of what he called the "white moderate."

"I have almost reached the regrettable conclusion that the Negro's great stumbling block in his stride toward freedom is not the White Citizen's Counciler or the Ku Klux Klanner, but the white moderate," King wrote, "who is more devoted to 'order' than to justice; who prefers a negative peace which is the absence of tension to a positive peace which is the presence of justice; who constantly says: 'I agree with you in the goal you seek, but I cannot agree with your methods of direct action'; who paternalistically believes he can set the timetable for another man's freedom; who lives by a mythical concept of time and who constantly advises the Negro to wait for a 'more convenient season.' Shallow understanding from people of good will is more frustrating than absolute misunderstanding from people of ill will. Lukewarm acceptance is much more bewildering than outright rejection."

King also said that he had wept at the "laxity" of the church. "If today's church does not capture the sacrificial spirit of the early church," he wrote, "it will lose its authenticity, forfeit the loyalty of millions and be dismissed as irrelevant social club with no meaning for the twentieth century."

Now, two years later on the morning of March 20, 1965, seeing no sign of cooperation from Carpenter or the leadership of St. Paul's in Selma, Rev. Myers, the suffragan bishop of Michigan, led a group of about two hundred would-be worshippers to the church but were blocked at the entrance by the police. There, the group—consisting mainly of ESCRU members and supporters—recited the penitential office from the Episcopal Prayer Book and then walked silently back to Brown Chapel, where Myers celebrated communion on a makeshift altar set up on the sidewalk—a gesture designed to symbolize, he said, the presence of Christ in temporal affairs.[47]

The presence of hundreds of "outside" clergy in Selma, in fact, underscored the failure of the white clergy in the South to deal with the race issue as the overwhelming majority of southern ministers, priests, and rabbis put their traditional way of life above any potential improvement in the lives of African Americans.

A year and a half earlier, a delegation sent to Selma by the National Council of Churches (NCC), in fact, would find only one kindred soul who shared its interest in promoting dialogue between the city's black and white communities: Father Maurice Ouellet, a Catholic priest of the Society of St. Edmund.

Ouellet was the only white clergy member in Selma who publicly supported the civil rights movement, and for his stance on race issues, he was constantly harassed by white residents, as well as by then-mayor Chris Heinz, who urged him to move out of the city. But Archbishop Thomas J. Toolen, of the Catholic Archdiocese of Mobile-Birmingham, rejected a request to transfer the Ouellet to another city, asking him instead to stop his "secular" activities.[48]

Another attempt at mediation came from the Reverend Ralph E. Smeltzer, a Church of Brethren pastor from Elgin, Illinois. Traveling to Selma in 1963, however, he received a hostile reception from his fellow Christians, including the pastor of Selma's largest Methodist church, George Kerlin, and the church congregation, which Smeltzer called a bastion of segregationists and strong supporters of Alabama Governor George C. Wallace.

Smeltzer found Rev. Matthews of St. Paul's to be what he called a "congenial back-slapper" but also someone who was opposed to "outside people" coming to Selma and "whipping people up." Historically, according to Smeltzer, quoting Matthews, there had never been any racial tension in Selma; in fact, Smeltzer said, Matthews claimed that Selma "really has no racial problem."[49]

Later, Matthews wrote in St. Paul's church bulletin that calm would only return to Selma when "troublesome immigrants have packed their bags and gathered their photographers and reporters and have left to wreak havoc in some other unsuspecting community."[50]

The Selma-to-Montgomery marchers, meanwhile, continued to make their way through rain and mud in Lowndes County, with Andrew Young now in charge on the third day of the march, March 23, having replaced Martin Luther King Jr., who had flown to Cleveland for a speaking engagement.

"The rain has made it difficult for the trucks to get out of last night's bivouac," Joseph Califano, of the Defense Department, reported back to Washington, DC, at 10:00 a.m. "One latrine truck is still stuck…The group is orderly; there have been no incidents." At 11:05 a.m., he continued, the marchers had crossed the intersection of US Highway 80 and Route 97, about sixteen miles west of the Montgomery city limit.

Most of the marchers, whose number was limited at this point to three hundred (which did not include us) in compliance with a federal court order restricting the number of marchers on the two-lane road portion of US Highway 80 through Lowndes County, wore ponchos made from large sheets of plastic. Hats were patched together from cereal boxes. But one of the government's representatives on the march—John M. Doar, head of the civil rights division at the Justice Department—was not so fortunate, as he walked through the torrential rain soaked to the skin. He said that the marchers did not complain about the rain but did raise objections over one state trooper who, they said, had been "high-handed" in directing traffic outside the campsite. Another trooper was heard to shout at an African American driver in a passing car, "Come on up over here, nigger."[51]

By 2:15 p.m., the marchers had closed in on their campsite for the night: a high-ground pasture near the junction of US Highway 80 and Route 21, which the FBI said in a report was a "sea of mud."

We were not aware at the time—but would learn later—that the farmland was owned by A. G. Gaston, a remarkable African American entrepreneur from Birmingham and a strong but silent supporter of the civil rights movement. At the time of his death in 1996 at 103 years old, he was reported to have been worth more than $130 million.

Gaston was born into poverty in the small town of Demopolis, Alabama, the son of a railroad worker and a woman who cooked for a prominent white family. When he was thirteen, his family moved to Birmingham, where his mother worked for A. B. Loveman, a wealthy Jewish department store owner, whose work ethic and attention to saving and investing later would become a model for the rising African American entrepreneur.

After serving in the army in World War I, Gaston earned a living as a coal miner in Fairfield, Alabama. His success at selling box lunches made by his mother to his fellow miners led him to sell popcorn and peanuts on the side and eventually to loan money to his fellow workers.

Soon, Gaston would establish a funeral service—the Booker T. Washington Burial Society—and sponsor gospel singers and Alabama's first regular African American radio program. Over time, he would branch out into other ventures, including a business college, a bottling company, a savings and loan association, a construction firm, and the A. G. Gaston Motel. In the late 1950s and early 1960s, civil rights leaders including King and Abernathy rented out the best suite at the motel at reduced rates to use as a war room for planning protests. And in retaliation, a bomb most likely planted by white segregationists blew off the motel's facade in 1963 (the same year that Gaston put up $160,000 to bail out King from a Birmingham jail).

At the Selma-to-Montgomery campsite on Gaston's property, just south of US Highway 80, several tents had already been erected by the time the marchers arrived. But the field was a quagmire. Hay was brought in to soak up some of the water. And security—such as it was—had broken down.

At last the rain stopped, and air mattresses were distributed. A small American flag was planted in front of one of the tents. "It looked so good to me," recalled Unitarian minister Richard D. Leonard from New York City, "that I put my mattress down close to it and spent many minutes just contemplating it."

Leonard said he slept from 8:00 p.m. to 1:30 a.m. and then in fits and starts until around 5:00 a.m. when the sky began to brighten. "As I sat on my mattress and looked out on the sea of mud," he said, "and realized that I would eventually have to climb back into cold, wet socks and barely recognizable shoes, open at the soles and caked with mud, for another fifteen-mile walk, perhaps in the rain, I had no trouble identifying with Job in the Old Testament sitting on his dung heap and asking why he was born."[52]

The Alabama State Legislature, for its part, decided to weigh in later in the day, adopting a series of resolutions denouncing the march and its participants. One resolution said that there had been evidence—vehemently denied by the participants in the march—of "much fornication" among the demonstrators and that "young women are returning to their respective states apparently as unwed expectant mothers." Another resolution—also scoffed at angrily by the marchers—said that "supposedly religious leaders from other parts of the United States" had been "drinking strong drink promiscuously" and using "vulgar language."[53]

That evening, Martin Luther King Jr. addressed an audience of 2,200 paying guests in Cleveland, telling them that the money being raised would be used to help defray the $50,000 cost for the Selma-to-Montgomery march. He also said that after ensuring enactment of the

Voting Rights Act of 1965 later in the year, he would begin to protest the "unjust conditions" of race nationwide, outside of the South.[54]

"We must act now before it is too late," King said at a dinner in his honor at the Hotel Sheraton-Cleveland. "We cannot afford not to live up to the American dream…[W]e all must learn to live together as brothers or all perish together as fools."

The "real heroes" of the civil rights struggle, he said, were those participating in the Selma-to-Montgomery voting rights march.[55]

It was just after midnight when King boarded a charter flight back to Alabama to rejoin the march, which was still slated to end at the state capitol in Montgomery on Thursday, March 25.

CHAPTER 7

The Trouble with Success

By the time I was moved to head south to join the Selma-to-Montgomery march, in March 1965, hundreds of white students and other activists—many from the North—had been working in the civil rights movement for years.

Among them were SNCC members Bob Zellner, Bill Hansen, John Perdew, Dotty Miller, Peter de Lissovoy, Constance Curry, Casey Hayden, and Sam Shirah, along with Zev Aelony of CORE and Anne Braden of the Southern Conference Educational Fund (SCEF), a small New Orleans-based civil rights group whose laudable but nearly impossible task was to solicit support among white southerners for the cause.

For some, notoriety would come but for wrong reasons: Michael Schwerner and Andrew Goodman, for example, were murdered by members of the Ku Klux Klan near Philadelphia, Mississippi, along with James Chaney, an African American, in June 1964.

Loners, too, would also seek to shake things up, like William L. Moore, a white postal worker from Baltimore who walked across Mississippi carrying signs protesting racial discrimination. He was shot to death on a road near Attalla, Alabama, in April 1963.

As for me, my first visit to the South came in the spring of 1962 when I volunteered to work at the Back Bay Mission in Biloxi, Mississippi—founded in 1922 as an outreach initiative of the First Evangelical Church (later the United Church of Christ). Its mission was to serve the impoverished and marginalized residents of the city, black and white.

But like other "do-gooder" organizations, the Back Bay Mission was also inescapably, and almost daily, involved in the ongoing struggle against racism and the institutions that nurtured it.

As a volunteer from the North, I was quickly introduced to the uncomfortable workings of the state of Mississippi by people like the Reverend Richard P. Ellerbrake, who ran the mission while I was there.

Just twenty-eight years old, Ellerbrake had been an advocate on behalf of racial equality as pastor of St. Paul's United Church of Christ in Biloxi. He was also a member of the Mississippi Advisory Committee to the US Commission on Civil Rights, and in that role he railed ceaselessly against the Mississippi State Sovereignty Commission, created by the Mississippi legislature in 1956 to defend the state against "encroachment" by the federal government and to portray the state-backed policy of racial segregation in a favorable light.

But over time, the commission also became a vehicle for a much more nefarious campaign: employing investigators and informants to disrupt civil rights activities across the state. One expert on its activities said that from 1956 to 1973 it "spied on civil rights workers, acted as a clearinghouse for information on civil rights activities and legislation from around the nation, funneled money to pro-segregation causes and distributed right-wing propaganda" (Sarah Rowe-Sims).

Unlike the KKK, however, it rejected the use of violence to achieve its objectives. Yet for five critical years—from 1960 to 1964—it provided funding for the White Citizens' Council, a white supremacist organization that incited violence and pursued the agenda of the KKK "with the demeanor of the Rotary [Club]," as one historian put it.[56]

Its interest in Ellerbrake was triggered by a letter he had sent to its director, Albert Jones, in which he objected to the commission's decision to allocate $20,000 in public funds to the White Citizens' Council. He called the decision a flagrant violation of the democratic principle that public funds should only be used "for that which is in the best interest of the public."

"Roughly half of Mississippi's 'public' are colored citizens," Ellerbrake wrote in the letter, dated July 8, 1960. "I doubt that they approve such an expenditure; nor do many intelligent white citizens, who see in it only the continued foment of discord and group hatred upon the people of Mississippi."

On July 11, after receiving the letter, Jones telephoned the mayor of Biloxi, Laz Quave, and asked him what he knew about Ellerbrake.

"[Quave] stated that Rev. Ellerbrake was very definitely an integrationist and persistent in his efforts to bring about equality among the races," according to an internal commission memo that Jones wrote about his conversation with Quave. "Mayor Quave stated that he thought [Ellerbrake] came to Biloxi, Mississippi, from the State of Minnesota. Mayor Quave stated that he had nothing to do with Rev. Ellerbrake, in any manner."

Jones also reported that he had spoken with Howard McDonald, a member of St. Paul's congregation, who said that he did not know Ellerbrake but that he had "very little respect for Ellerbrake's ideas regarding segregation."

Jesse E. Stockstill, a fellow member of the commission, urged Jones to reply to the letter from Ellerbrake and drafted a possible response. It condemned Ellerbrake for embracing "leanings to nefarious Communistic Organizations that are sweeping this Nation…"

Stockstill, a seventy-six-year-old attorney from Picayune, Mississippi, argued that *Brown v. Board of Education*, the 1954 Supreme Court decision that struck down state segregation of public schools, was a "farcical undertaking to force the wholesale mixing of Negro and white races in schools, transportation facilities, public parks, hotels, restaurants, and all other facilities which have been segregated heretofore for 95 years…"

The aim of segregation, Stockstill wrote, had been to protect the "pure White Anglo-Saxon blood of the people of America," to maintain a "safe degree of health for the inhabitants of the Nation (now sacrificing the millions of dollars spent by the States to eradicate venereal disease among

the Negroes, as well as cases where they have transmitted it to Whites),"
and to ultimately prevent the "downfall and degradation of the pure
White races of this Nation from the inevitable miscegenation that will
surely be inflicted upon all inhabitants, including all races, which will be
to the everlasting decline and final downfall as a Nation."

Other members of the commission, however, while agreeing with the
sentiments expressed in the Stockstill draft, were against sending the letter, arguing that it could be used in a lawsuit contesting the commission's
decision to allocate money to the White Citizens' Council, so it was never
sent.

In the end, the commission decided not to take action against
Ellerbrake. But eventually he would be forced to resign as pastor of St.
Paul's, in the summer of 1962, in the wake of mounting pressure from
the church membership over his association with the US Civil Rights
Commission.

Yet the Mississippi State Sovereignty Commission continued to
thrive, receiving $50,000 in appropriations from the state legislature for
the two-year period ending June 30, 1964—meaning that the taxpaying
African American residents of Mississippi were being forced to support an
organization whose aim was to repress them economically, socially, and
politically.

It is not surprising, given the times, that other southern states, nota-
bly Louisiana and Alabama, would use the Mississippi commission as a
model for creating similar institutions to fight racial integration and the
"encroachment" of the federal government in their affairs. Cooperation
among the three states—Mississippi, Louisiana, and Alabama—was for-
malized with the founding of the Southern Association of Investigators in
1966 and the Interstate Sovereignty Commission in 1968.

Local white pro-integration advocates like Ellerbrake continued to
play a role in the movement. But in the summer of 1964, their work
was overshadowed by the invasion of more than a thousand out-of-state
volunteers who had been recruited to participate in a ten-week voter

registration drive in Mississippi. Ninety percent of the participants were white, and most of them were young and from the North. It was in those early days of what has since become known as "Freedom Summer," in fact, that Schwerner, Goodman, and Chaney were murdered.

The groundwork for initiative, however, had been laid earlier. At the third annual general conference of SNCC, held April 27–29, 1962, for instance, some 250 delegates and observers from twenty-two states gathered in Atlanta, Georgia, to discuss broadening the work of the organization beyond campus protest activities to community organizing and voter registration. Nearly one-third of the participants at that meeting were white.[57]

By 1963, white activists had begun to play a wider and more important leadership role in the movement, with the hiring, for example, of Casey Hayden and Mary E. King to expand SNCC's publicity operations—two years after Bob Zellner had become the first white southerner to be named a SNCC field secretary.[58]

Charles Sherrod, an African American project director for SNCC, argued that using whites as voter registration volunteers was necessary "to strike at the very root of segregation...the idea that white is superior...We can only [break that image] if [local blacks] see white and black people working together, side by side, the white man no more and no less than his black brother, but human beings together."

Others in the movement, however, disagreed, saying that there were already too many white people in the movement.

Hollis Watkins, a SNCC staffer, reflected the views of many when he said that whites coming from the North to Mississippi would destroy the grassroots civil rights institutions that were being built by the local population.

"For the first time," he said, "we had local people who had begun to take the initiative themselves and do things. For the first time, we had local Mississippians who were making decisions....We felt that with a lot of students from the North coming in, being predominantly white, that they would come in and overshadow the grassroots organizations..."[59]

Finding room for a relatively small number of individual white volunteers in the movement was not difficult, and by the fall of 1963 about 20 percent of SNCC's staff was white. But sending large numbers of white students into black communities that historically had feared and distrusted whites, in the "Freedom Summer" of 1964, was another matter.

"At this point," according to a SNCC report, written in 1963, "it is too dangerous for whites to participate in the project in Mississippi—too dangerous for them and too dangerous for the Negroes who would be working with them."

The report also cited the "higher pitch" of "terror" in Mississippi than in nearby Georgia, saying that "this means not only more outright violence but more difficulty in obtaining a place to meet and more difficulty in convincing local leaders (ministers, teachers, doctors, and other professionals) to take an active stand."

Even in Georgia, according to Anne Braden, white workers were running into problems in black communities because of their race. White students, she said in December 1962, did not have "an easy time communicating with Negroes who have known whites only as oppressors." John Perdew of SNCC said that poor blacks were frequently "afraid of me as a white."

Yet plans to import one thousand-plus northern white volunteers to Mississippi in the summer of 1964—drafted by SNCC project director Bob Moses and Allard K. Lowenstein, a white activist from New York—were, nevertheless, set quickly into motion.

Moses argued that the only hope for blacks was to change the power structure in Mississippi by provoking a crisis between the federal government and the state government. That could only be done, he argued, by swamping the state with out-of-state volunteers. His assumption was that the state alone would not be able crush such a massive show of force and, moreover, that public opinion nationwide would not tolerate law enforcement assaults against defenseless white students.

But the Council of Confederated Organizations (COFO), a loose coalition of major civil rights organizations, decided in November 1963 to recruit only one hundred northern white students for the "Freedom Summer" project, despite a plea from COFO codirector Moses that to have white people "working alongside of you...changes the whole complexion of what you're doing, so it isn't any longer Negro fighting white, it's a question of rational people against irrational people...I always thought that the one thing we can do for the country that no one else can do is to be above the race issue."[60]

Support for the project, meanwhile, continued to grow, with Lowenstein and others formulating plans of their own to bring thousands of students to Mississippi in the summer of 1964 to force a showdown between state and federal officials. The National Council of Churches was also planning to organize its own projects. And John Lewis, who had been elected chairman of SNCC in June 1963, said that SNCC wanted to create such a crisis in Mississippi that the federal government would have to intervene. "Out of this conflict, this division and chaos," he said, "will come something positive."[61]

Finding white students in the North who were willing to spend their summer in the dangerous South was, perhaps surprisingly, not at all difficult.

"They all wanted to come to where the action was," said Casey Hayden, who had moved to Mississippi in 1963 to work for SNCC. "These were the early sixties. Kids on college campuses were reading existentialists. The black students were... like existentialist heroes...They wanted to get close to it."[62]

Hayden's husband at the time—the activist Tom Hayden, who also worked in Mississippi—has said that, for the leaders of the civil rights movement, the aim was to "mobilize the North" to put pressure on

Congress and the administration, so that "they would finally do something about these strongholds of segregation in the South."

"The conclusion was that...it would be necessary to bring down the white sons and daughters of the country's middle class from the liberal North," Hayden said, "to experience the true nature of southern segregation."[63]

Bob Zellner, of SNCC, noting that "only" one white person (William L. Moore, the postal worker from Baltimore) had been killed fighting for civil rights in the South prior to June 1964, explained it this way: "We knew that if black people were brutalized and arrested, neither the country nor the government was going to care. But if the son of white lawyer so-and-so or the daughter of white senator such-and-such got beaten or arrested—or God forbid, killed—people would have to pay attention and demand that the government do something about it...We would have to pull out all the stops. A thousand volunteers from middle-class families, black and white, from all over the United States would converge on Mississippi. That would get attention and possibly protection for people attempting to register to vote."[64]

For many of us in the North, however, the decision to travel south to participate in the civil rights movement had little to do with strategy or existentialism. Rather, it was a visceral response to racial injustice. The murder of fellow white activists like Schwerner and Goodman touched a nerve. But the violence being perpetrated daily against African Americans was, of course, even more troubling.

News of one case, in particular, spoke to us like no other.

It involved Louis Allen, an African American logger from Liberty, Mississippi, who in September 1961 had witnessed what he claimed initially was the killing in self-defense of another African American and fellow voter registration activist, Herbert Lee, by a white state legislator, E. H. Hurst.

Amite County Sheriff E. L. Caston said at the time that he and other local officials had investigated the incident and found, according to the

Mississippi State Sovereignty Commission, that Lee had attempted to attack Hurst with an eighteen-inch tire iron, which prompted Hurst to strike Lee on the head with his .38-caliber revolver. The gun discharged, according to Allen and the others, killing Lee instantly.

A coroner's jury the same day cleared Hurst after hearing testimony from five witnesses—two whites and three African Americans, including Allen. A hearing at the county courthouse on September 26 also exonerated Hurst after it had taken testimony from the same five witnesses, ruling that he had acted in self-defense.

But Allen later told SNCC activists Julian Bond and Bob Moses that he had falsified his testimony out of fear for his life. "If he had implicated a powerful white man in a murder of a black man," Bond said years later, "he was risking his life...I tried to encourage him to tell the truth, but it was like saying 'Why don't you volunteer to be killed?'"

Eventually, Allen decided to approach the FBI, saying that in reality, Hurst had shot Lee without provocation. Word of what Allen had done spread quickly through Liberty's white population. He was threatened repeatedly and even shot once and beaten by the county's newly elected sheriff, Daniel Jones. Again fearing for his life, Allen decided to escape to Milwaukee to move in with relatives. But on the night before he was scheduled to leave—January 31, 1964—he was ambushed at his property outside Liberty and killed by two shotgun blasts to the head. No charges were filed at the time.

Since then, the FBI has reopened the case following an investigation by Tulane University history professor Plater Robinson, and Jones has been targeted as the prime suspect. But again, no charges have been filed.

News of Allen's murder spread rapidly to the dormitories of mainly white colleges and universities in the North. It underscored the gravity of the situation, but it also reminded the students of what dangers lay ahead.

Peter Orris, a freshman at Harvard University, said that he and the other white students who attended training sessions at Western College for Women in Oxford, Ohio, in mid-June 1964 spent hours listening to

Bob Moses and other SNCC leaders "give us a feeling of exactly what kind of a tense atmosphere we were going into, what kind of violence we should expect, how to avoid violence, as well as nonviolent responses to violent situations."[65]

Many white Mississippians, of course, were resentful of "outsiders" coming into the state (where in 1962, incidentally, only 6.2 percent of eligible African American voters were registered to vote) to fundamentally change their way of life. They regularly harassed the volunteers with drive-by shootings and Molotov cocktails—all with the implicit (and sometimes explicit) support of the local authorities.

In the end—after ten weeks of voter registration work and the creation of Freedom Schools and community centers in small towns throughout the state—about 17,000 African Americans were moved enough to fill out voter registration forms, but only 1,600 were permitted to register.[66] Four civil rights workers had been killed. A total of eighty Freedom Summer workers were beaten. At least three African Americans from Mississippi who supported the project were murdered. Thirty-seven churches were bombed or burned. And thirty African American homes or businesses were attacked.

Most observers, however, said that the project had been a success, arguing that it had, after all, generated widespread press coverage nationally, which, for the movement, was unprecedented. Quite literally, according to one study, its triumph could be measured in column inches of newsprint and running feet of videotape. "Easily the most spectacular and sustained single event in recent civil rights history," the study said, "it provided summer-long, nationwide exposure of the inequities of white supremacy in the deepest of the Deep South states."[67]

But Bob Moses, who had played a pivotal role in initiating and executing the project, was not convinced that it had been worth it. "Success?" he told a group of reporters. "I have trouble with that word. When we started, we hoped no one would be killed."[68]

CHAPTER 8

A Sea of Mud

It was a brisk and sunny morning as the marchers set off just after 7:00 a.m. on Wednesday, March 24—the fourth day of the five-day march from Selma to Montgomery.

After having spent the night camped in a field at the Gaston farm just south of US Highway 80, about twenty miles west of Montgomery, they were joined by hundreds of others as they closed in slowly on the Alabama state capital. And I was one of them.

I had marched with about three thousand other protestors on the first day of the march and, with all but three hundred of them, had returned to Selma that evening to wait until now, when we would be allowed to rejoin the march as US Highway 80 widened to four lanes and the limit on the number of marchers was lifted. By late morning, there were about twelve hundred of us; by midafternoon, we were four to five thousand.

Califano, of the Defense Department, wrote in a dispatch filed back to Washington, DC, at 10:00 a.m. that the only notable incident that morning involved the driver of a support vehicle who had been been punched in the nose after stopping at a gas station run by whites. A small contingent of national guardsmen, Califano said, had been sent to the scene to investigate.

Throughout the afternoon, cars and buses discharged new marchers along the route. A brief but heavy rain shower soaked everyone. But we were in a jubilant mood, singing freedom songs as we passed a billboard with large letters exhorting citizens to "Help Get the U.S. Out of the United Nations."

Animosity among the local population toward the march and the marchers, in the meantime, continued to grow.

The city of Selma, for instance, filed a lawsuit against Martin Luther King Jr. and other "nonresident" civil rights leaders seeking $100,000 in damages for the loss of revenue resulting from the boycott of the city buses and the police protection needed in the weeks of civil rights demonstrations leading up to the march.

"We believe that a court of law is a proper forum for the settlement of just grievances," Selma Mayor Joe T. Smitherman said, "and not the streets and highways of our city and state."

J. A. Pickard, the city's superintendent of schools, attacked "outside agitators" for causing a sharp drop in attendance at R. B. Hudson High School and other segregated African American schools in the city.

"The effects of the demonstrations in and around Selma during the past weeks have been devastating to the Negro schools of the Selma City School System," Pickard said. "Particularly in the early days of the movement, students defied their parents and school teachers by participating in demonstrations. After constant harangue by outside agitators, many parents and their children no longer realize that they must work and study to better themselves, but expect to be given privileges, normally earned through considerable effort, purely because they demonstrate."

A. R. Meadows, the Alabama state superintendent of education, said that parents would be fined $100 and sentenced to hard labor for up to ninety days for failing to send their children to school.

One Selma resident said in a letter to the editor in *The Selma Times-Journal* that the religious leaders who had come to the city from other parts of the country were participating in, as he put it, "one of the greatest fiascoes ever witnessed in America—the march to Montgomery to secure rights which have already been granted."

"Like a Ringling Brothers circus parade with its menagerie of clowns, clergymen, politicians and beatniks with everything but a calliope," the reader wrote, "they will march down Highway 80...They have not bound together a divided community, but have driven its citizens further apart. They have not manifest a spirit of love but of judgement...Some day they will leave. They will have eased their consciences, satisfied their flair for the dramatic, and inflated their egos. But they leave behind a community and a church sorely wounded by what they did and did not do. And upon us...will fall the responsibility of trying to build back and restore a community spirit of love and understanding and brotherhood which they helped to destroy."

Nationally, news magazines and religious journals reported favorably on what they saw as a new brand of social activism among the nation's clergy. But some condemned their involvement. A young Baptist minister and the future founder of the Moral Majority, Jerry Falwell, told his parishioners at the Thomas Road Baptist Church in Lynchburg, Virginia, that preaching the gospel of Jesus Christ was a full-time job. He said that minsters were not called by God to be politicians but to be "soul winners."[69]

Along the route of the march as we approached Montgomery, I saw fewer and fewer white men and women protesting our presence—perhaps because the *Montgomery Advertiser* had run an ad by the City Commissioner's Committee on Community Affairs calling on local residents to ignore the march and not overreact.

For his part, Richard D. Leonard, a thirty-seven-year-old Unitarian minister from New York City, who had marched now for three days, was becoming concerned about the "gruesome appearance I was presenting as a minister," as cars and buses continued to drop off "cleanly scrubbed" passengers (like me) to join the hike on day four. He had not shaved or changed shirts and was not able to get a comb through his matted hair. But he was heartened at the news that large numbers of people from around the country were due to arrive in Montgomery later in the day to join the final leg of the march, set for Thursday, March 25.[70]

One of the more committed activists on the march was Casey Hayden, a cofounder of SNCC, who, according to those who knew her, was simple, gentle, and very southern, with impeccable manners. She was deeply concerned about social issues and seemed to know instinctively what was right, they said.[71]

She was also married to the high-profile, left-wing activist Tom Hayden. The couple, who "sparkled together,"[72] met for the first time at a meeting of the National Student Association (NSA) in 1960 and again at a SNCC conference in Atlanta later that year. From the beginning, she was a supporter of what was called in SNCC's founding document the "philosophical or religious idea" of nonviolence as the "foundation of our purpose, the presupposition of our belief and the manner of our action."

"My life in the sixties was strewn with crowded overnight car trips and red-eye airplane flights," she wrote later. "I and others like me moved fast and improvised, carrying ideas and names and contacts, connecting folks to each other, welding, one by one, those crucial linkages. We moved so fast the dross burned off. We burned down to our essential selves, and our relationships were intense. I was part of a small group who were the tip of the wedge of change, carrying the weight of opening space for all who came after us."[73]

At SNCC's leadership conference in March 1962, she and Bob Zellner had organized a workshop on the role of white students in the movement. "I liked the leverage white students would provide," she wrote later. "Press and northern politicians would pay attention."[74]

But by 1965, SNCC had entered a period of transition—from a nonviolent, interracial organization to a more militant, Afro-centric institution.

"I watched, conflicted and depressed, as that fabric unraveled," Casey Hayden wrote. Tensions were on the rise between whites who still believed in interracial cooperation and blacks who were seeking their own identity.

Hayden said she listened to SNCC Chairman John Lewis at a SNCC conference in Atlanta in February 1965, where he indicated that what the organization needed was not more whites but black leaders who were strong, militant, and experienced.[75]

After the Selma-to-Montgomery march, while she continued to draw her paycheck from SNCC of $9.64 a week, she left for Cleveland, and eventually Chicago, to work with the Economic Research and Action Project (ERAP)—an initiative created by Students for a Democratic Society (SDS) to organize poor whites in urban areas.

"I was trying to follow the new [segregated] line in SNCC," Hayden wrote, "viewing my move as an experimental effort to find ways for whites to leave SNCC and work on the white side. I hoped for an alliance now between black and white, even though we were working in separate communities."

But now, at midafternoon on the fourth day of the march, the "separate communities" we were part of were still working closely together, arriving tired but exuberant at the City of St. Jude—a Catholic-run complex with a church, hospital and school—where we would stay the night before concluding the march the next day by walking several miles to the state capitol in Montgomery.

After having flown to Cleveland to speak the previous night, Martin Luther King Jr. had rejoined the march, and walking behind him was the Reverend Morris H. Tynes from Chicago, who joked with his friend as they walked. "Moses, can you let your people rest for a minute?" Tynes asked. "Can you just let the homiletic smoke from your cigarette drift out of your mouth and engulf the multitude and let them rest?"

Years later I would come across a letter written by Tynes—and signed by King, along with several other civil rights leaders—calling on high school and college students, through their churches and synagogues, to travel to Washington, DC, on April 18, 1959, to demonstrate in support of the "immediate and peaceful integration of the schools of our nation."

An estimated 26,000 had heeded the call, marching down the National Mall that day and demanding, in the words of their petition, that the president and Congress put into effect an "executive and legislative program which will insure the orderly and speedy integration of schools throughout the United States."

Learning about that event was a reminder to me of how long the struggle for racial justice in the United States had been going on—well before I and many others had gotten involved. Some say that the origins of the movement as an organized force date back to the Montgomery bus boycott of 1955–1956 and to the refusal of Rosa Parks to give up her seat to a white man. Others, like Danielle L. McGuire, in the remarkable book *At the Dark End of the Street*, have argued that the beginning of the movement dates back to 1944 when Parks, an organizer for the NAACP, was sent to Abbeville, Alabama, to investigate the rape of a twenty-four-year-old mother and sharecropper by seven white men armed with knives and shotguns.

Now, twenty-one years later, on March 24, 1965, newspapers across the country were reporting on the war in Vietnam and the successful flight of the Gemini 3 spacecraft, as well as the Selma-to-Montgomery march. Not surprisingly, *The Selma Times-Journal* devoted considerable space to the march and the reaction to it, particularly among the local white population.

It reported, for instance, that Representative William L. Dickinson (R), a member of Congress from Montgomery, had asked Governor George C. Wallace to receive the marchers "courteously and graciously" when they arrived at the state capitol on March 25. Otherwise, he said, "these thousands of civil rights demonstrators may decide to camp by the thousands indefinitely on the capitol grounds, getting more and more publicity for Martin Luther King at the expense of the state and the people of Alabama in the process." He said that Wallace should tell the marchers, "as he has many times told the rest of the nation," that anyone who is qualified to register to vote can vote in Alabama.

A Detroit resident said in a letter to the editor of *The Selma Times-Journal* that he would like to apologize to the residents of Selma for the behavior of his fellow northerners, calling them "jackasses wandering around the countryside with blinders on."

"I must side with Governor Wallace and [Dallas County] Sheriff [Jim] Clark in demanding that the Northern church and political do-gooders return to their own troubled areas in the North," the writer, Jerry Woodman, said. "I'm sorry for all the Yankee agitation that has caused so much trouble in such a pleasant Southern city as Selma."

One Selma resident—Ella Holladay Harris—urged all Americans to write to President Johnson protesting what she called the "discrimination now being leveled against Alabama."

But the newspaper also published an AP story noting that the Ralph D. Abernathy, a top aide to Martin Luther King Jr., had told journalists that he considered the Selma-to-Montgomery march to be the "greatest demonstration for freedom in the nation since Abraham Lincoln signed the Emancipation Proclamation"—an exaggeration perhaps, but nonetheless heartfelt.

It had been raining off and on during the day, so when we arrived at the City of St. Jude on the outskirts of Montgomery after several hours of walking along US Highway 80, the field where we would camp for the night was now deep in mud. One hiker described the experience as an adventure in "mud skiing." Thousands poured into the grounds from Selma and Montgomery through lax security, planning to march the final few miles the next day. And now, instead of being subjected to jeers and insults from white segregationists along the route, we were being cheered by people on both sides of the street in the African American section of the city.

No one seemed to know exactly who had given us permission to use the St. Jude grounds for our final campsite that night. It was certainly not the Catholic Church as an institution, since its leaders were far from united on the question of employing church resources in the campaign for social justice, which included, of course, the Selma-to-Montgomery march.

We had heard that Father Paul J. Mullaney, the director of St. Jude, had said that the permission had come from Archbishop Thomas J. Toolen, which seemed odd, if not unlikely, given his longstanding and very public opposition to the march.

Toolen's record on race was mixed. A year earlier, as schools in Alabama continued to oppose implementing the Supreme Court's 1954 decision striking down state laws establishing separate schools for black and white students, Toolen took the bold step, which angered many white parents, of desegregating all Catholic schools in Alabama, effective immediately. But he also denounced the tactics of civil rights protestors, saying that "outsiders" like the dozens of Catholic priests and nuns who had come to Selma from New York, Michigan, and other states were just there to stir up trouble.

Still, parishioners at St. Elizabeth's Church in Selma—under the leadership of Father Ouellet, of the Edmundite order—continued to work closely and proudly with SNCC, housing and feeding visiting marchers and carrying on a tradition initiated by Edmundites of working in Selma on behalf of the city's African American community for nearly thirty years by building, for example, a hospital and a school dedicated to their care and education.

Ouellet's superior, the Very Reverend Eymard Galligan, had decided in the fall of 1963 that he wanted the Edmundites to play a more active role in Selma, particularly in promoting racial integration, so he wrote to Toolen saying he hoped that the Edmundites would be allowed to "actively help the Negro people in their struggle, knowing full well the dangers involved and the consequences." But Toolen replied by saying that picketing and marching by all priests and nuns in his diocese was and would remain strictly prohibited.

Yet the struggle within the Catholic Church over the race issue would continue. A month before the Selma-to-Montgomery march, in February 1965, Father John Crowley, director of the Edmundites' southern missions, took out a full-page ad in *The Selma Times-Journal* citing the "evils" of racial discrimination and insisting on the need for street protests to remedy the situation.

"[Racial discrimination] denies to a citizen his human and civil rights," Crowley wrote, "and thus undermines the principles on which our nation was founded...Fair-minded citizens reject the evils of segregation."

The Edmundite leader argued that the United States was "fortunate" to have African American leaders in its midst who were, he said, by and large "temperate" and dedicated to American ideals.

"It is when their so-obviously just claims are ignored, their needs completed unattended, their just demands refused," the Catholic cleric wrote, "that the streets become their only means of protest. The Negroes in Selma...have no other power...That is why we support wholeheartedly those non-violent efforts to obtain their full rights as Americans."

Archbishop Toolen blew up, firing off a letter to Father Galligan saying that he and the Edmundite Fathers had come to a "parting of the ways."

"Both Crowley and Ouellet have shot off their mouths entirely too much," he wrote. "I have put up with as much as I am going to...I have always felt closer to the Edmundite Fathers than any other Community in the Diocese, but Selma has cured this." He said he wanted Ouellet "out of Selma." And soon the man called by Martin Luther King Jr. the "most righteous white man in Selma" was gone.

CHAPTER 9

Anger Turned to Good

The mood among the dozens of celebrities on the short flight from Atlanta to Montgomery on the afternoon of March 24, 1965, was upbeat—but apprehensive.

Leonard Bernstein, the American conductor and composer, sat in the front. Behind him was Oscar-winning actress Shelley Winters, who joked with comedian Alan King. In the back of the plane James Baldwin and his brother David were silent. Across from them was Floyd Patterson—"The Gentleman of Boxing"—with Peter, Paul, and Mary munching on cold fried chicken and a salad behind him.

Waiting at the Montgomery airport to load the celebrities onto a bus for downtown and the Greystone Hotel, near the Alabama state capitol, was Ossie Davis, the actor and activist. In the lobby of the hotel, Harry Belafonte gestured wildly, assigning rooms to the other stars who had arrived earlier.

Over the course of the afternoon, more planes landed at Montgomery's Dannelly Field carrying more celebrities, including Tony Bennett, Sammy Davis Jr., Tony Perkins, Nina Simone, Bobby Darin, Mike Nichols, and Elaine May. After freshening up in their hotel rooms, they were off in two busloads to St. Jude's, where a "Stars for Freedom" rally—organized by Belafonte—would be held that night for the exhausted marchers and thousands of other supporters.[76]

Belafonte, who had just turned thirty-eight, was at the peak of his career. Dubbed the "King of Calypso," he had recorded his breakthrough album *Calypso* in 1956—the first LP to sell more than a million copies.

He was also the first African American to win an Emmy (1959) and had racked up other triumphs in Hollywood and on Broadway.

But his greatest achievement, he would say later, was his work as a civil rights activist. By March 1965, he had already been involved in the movement for more than a decade, appearing, for instance, with Duke Ellington at a fund-raising event in December 1956—"Salute to Montgomery"—and marching with Martin Luther King Jr. at countless freedom rallies across the country. In 1963, he helped organize the "March on Washington" (where King delivered his "I Have a Dream" speech on the steps of the Lincoln Memorial). And not insignificantly he provided critical financial backing for King's Southern Christian Leadership Conference (SCLC) and for SNCC, as well as for the entire King family, especially early on in their lives when, as a preacher, King was making only $8,000 a year and supporting a growing family.

"Whenever we got into trouble or when tragedy struck," King's wife, Coretta Scott King, later recalled, "Harry has always come to our aid, his generous heart wide open." He also raised thousands of dollars to bail out civil rights protesters, including King, and so concerned was he for the safety and well-being of the King family that he personally took out life insurance policies worth $100,000 each for each of his four children.[77]

But Belafonte's most dramatic and daring achievement came in the summer of 1964, following the murders of Michael Schwerner, James Chaney, and Andrew Goodman in Mississippi by the KKK.

It began in the evening of August 4, 1964, when the phone rang in Belafonte's twenty-one-room apartment on the Upper West Side of New York. "We've got a crisis on our hands down here," the man on the other end of the line, SNCC's James Forman, told him. "We need help."

The bodies of Schwerner, Chaney, and Goodman had just recently been found in a shallow grave near Philadelphia, Mississippi, which prompted many white students from the North who had taken part in the Freedom Summer not to leave the state, as might have been expected, but instead to request permission to stay longer to carry on the fight. But money was running short.

Forman told Belafonte that if the students were to leave Mississippi now, the KKK would claim that it had driven them out. "The press would play it that way," he said. "And if they all stay, we can get thousands of more voters registered. The problem is we don't have the resources to keep them all here." He said he needed at least $50,000, adding that he said he expected to burn through the meager remainder of his budget in the next seventy-two hours.

Belafonte had already opened his personal checkbook to the tune of about $50,000 to help establish SNCC a few years earlier, and he was prepared to do so again. But he recalled the experience of his idol, the singer, actor, and activist Paul Robeson, whose generosity on behalf of various social causes had almost ruined him financially. So Belafonte vowed to raise most of the money from outside sources—and quickly.

The Chicago newspaper columnist and broadcaster Irv Kupcinet offered to help by hosting a fund-raiser at his home, where rich Chicagoans would throw checks and cash at Belafonte on a hastily arranged visit to the Windy City totaling $35,000. A trip to Montreal yielded another $20,000, and he and his wife, Julie, collected an additional $15,000 at a fund-raiser at their apartment in New York.

Now, however, he had to figure out a way to get the money to Mississippi. "I couldn't just wire it and have a black activist go to the local Western Union office to ask for his [money], please," he said later. "He'd be dead before he drove a mile away. So would a white college volunteer... The money would have to be brought down in cash. And unless I could come up with a brighter idea, I'd have to take it down myself."

So Belafonte—failing to come up with a brighter idea—contacted his longtime friend and fellow entertainer Sidney Poitier, who was understandably reluctant to join him on his mission south. But Belafonte eventually convinced his friend, joking that while "the chances of a Klansman taking a potshot at me were actually pretty high...it'll be harder for them to knock off two black stars than one. Strength in numbers, man."

Unaccompanied, the two men then boarded a plane at the airport in Newark, New Jersey, for Jackson, Mississippi, toting a black doctor's bag filled with $70,000 in small bills.

At the Jackson airport, Forman and two SNCC volunteers met them and took them to a private airstrip with a dirt runway, where they were put on a small Cessna and flown by an unfriendly white pilot ("Was he a Klansman, leading us into a trap?") some one hundred miles north to Greenwood, Mississippi, where SNCC had its state headquarters.

Two more SNCC volunteers, in two cars, were waiting for them for the drive to town, and as they were starting their engines the driver of the car carrying Belafonte and Poitier—SNCC field secretary Willie Blue— saw a long row of headlights at the far end of the pitch-black airfield. "That's the Klan," he said. But instead of turning away, he and the driver of the other car drove full-speed toward the outline of three or four pickup trucks in the distance.

Nearing the trucks, the two SNCC cars then swung around to take an alternate route to town, and the trucks fell in line behind them. "Why aren't you driving faster?" Belafonte asked Blue, who was keeping strictly to the forty-five-mile-an-hour speed limit. "Faster, man!"

But Blue refused, saying he was not about to drive at full speed because that was exactly what the Klansmen wanted him to do. "They got a state trooper there waiting in his car with the headlights off, ready to arrest us for speeding," Blue said. "He takes us to the station, lets us out in an hour, and even more of the Klan be waiting for us. That's how they work. That's how those boys [Schwerner, Chaney, and Goodman] got killed."

Belafonte later recalled that one of the pickup trucks kept ramming the back of the car as Blue maneuvered his vehicle toward the middle of the two-lane road to keep the truck from pulling alongside. "We can't let them pull up beside us," Blue said. "They'll shoot."

After two or three "terrifying" minutes, which "seemed like forever," Belafonte said, a convoy of cars appeared ahead. "That's them," Blue said, signaling that a SNCC brigade was coming to the rescue. "My heart was still pounding, but I started to breathe again."

As the pickup trucks slowly retreated, a dozen or so shots rang out in the night air. But no one was hit, fortunately, and the SNCC convoy led the cars into Greenwood, where hundreds of SNCC volunteers had assembled at their headquarters in an old barn to greet Belafonte and Poitier.

"Screams of joy went up from the crowd," Belafonte recalled. "Sidney and I had heard a lot of applause in our day, but never anything like those cheers...To have two of the biggest black stars in the world walk in to show solidarity with them—that meant a lot to them, and to us."

He said that once the crowd had settled down, he held up the black satchel he had brought with him and turned it upside down on a table in front of him, letting bundles of cash roll out to the shouts of the roomful of tired but now-inspired and overjoyed SNCC volunteers.

Belafonte said that when he got home to his wife and children—waiting in the family's apartment in New York City—he asked himself why he had taken on the civil rights movement as his personal crusade.

"I knew the reason I'd gotten involved in general—any black American with a pulse and a conscience had done that by the summer of 1964," he wrote, "at least to the extent of writing the occasional check. A lot of white Americans had, too. All of us sensed this was a point at which history simply had to turn. We couldn't tolerate more lynchings and beatings. We couldn't abide more 'whites-only' signs on the hotels and restaurants and gas stations and water fountains and bus stations in the segregated South. We couldn't let black Americans be treated as slaves in all but name anymore."

This wasn't anything new, he said. Everyone knew that. "But why did I feel so personally offended?" he asked. His mother had much to do with it. Yet long after his initial involvement in the movement, he would continue to struggle with "piecing the parts together."

"Why this little boy, among all others, should use his anger to push himself up, make a name for himself, and then make it his mission to smash racial barriers and injustice with such grim determination, I'm not sure I can say," Belafonte wrote. "Perhaps, in the end, where your anger comes from is less important than what you do with it."[78]

CHAPTER 10

Stars Come Out for Freedom

What I remember most about the night of March 24, 1965—aside from the world-class, knockout entertainment that Harry Belafonte had arranged for us at the City of St. Jude outside Montgomery—was the mud. It was what Belafonte most remembered, too.

The megastar entertainer had succeeded in persuading many of his fellow entertainers to drop what they were doing and fly to Montgomery to perform at a "Stars for Freedom" rally on the last night of the Selma-to-Montgomery march. He had lined up transportation for them from the airport, and he found rooms for them at the majestic Greystone Hotel in downtown Montgomery, which boasted "circulating ice water, fans and bed lamps." All their expenses would be taken care of, he said, and they were.

"In all, that evening would cost me $10,000," Belafonte later wrote. "I could handle that. What I couldn't control was the rain."

By early evening, the temporary campsite that had been set up in the field directly behind the City of St. Jude was so inundated that the microphones and klieg lights that Belafonte had brought in kept sinking in the mud. A local teenager, however, came up with an idea that would save the day: retrieving a load of empty coffins from a local black funeral home, which were laid two rows deep in the mud, with a layer of plywood secured on the top, forming a makeshift stage. "Yes, *coffins*," John Lewis later recalled.[79]

Thousands of people, in fact, had found their way to St. Jude—mainly African Americans. And eventually, according to the US Justice Department, some thirty thousand would be on hand for the show.

In the darkness, I heard cries for help from people in the crush of humanity pressing against the stage. Several young girls collapsed and were lifted from the muddy field onto the lighted stage. Some two dozen people—none seriously ill or injured, thankfully—were carried off to the hospital on stretchers.

Finally, the entertainment—scheduled to begin at 9:00 p.m. but now two hours late—got under way as the jerry-built sound system suddenly came to life, with Belafonte opening the show with his calypso hit, "Jamaica Farewell."

The spectacle of two dozen or so "Stars for Freedom" now assembled on or near the makeshift stage was truly impressive and included, in addition to Belafonte, who emceed the proceedings, Tony Bennett, Sammy Davis Jr., Shelley Winters, Floyd Patterson, Nina Simone, Odetta, Nipsey Russell, Mike Nichols, Elaine May, Leonard Bernstein, Dick Gregory, and the Chad Mitchell Trio. They sang, told a joke or two, or just saluted to the crowd.

Simone sang "Mississippi Goddam," which she wrote in response to the murder of Medgar Evers in 1963. And Sammy Davis Jr., who had closed his Broadway show *Golden Boy* for the night to be in Montgomery, told the crowd after singing several songs that it was "the biggest thrill of my life" to be there.

Charles E. Fager, a participant in the Selma-to-Montgomery march who worked with King's Southern Christian Leadership Conference (SCLC), later wrote that "Montgomery that night had become the place to be and be seen..."[80]

The comedic team of Nichols and May offered the audience a sketch based on a "telegram" from Governor Wallace to President Johnson claiming he could not afford to call in state troops to protect the marchers because the cost of keeping hundreds of civil rights protesters in jail had grown so high, "to say nothing of the upkeep on cattle prods and bull whips."

For his part, Leonard Bernstein told the crowd he had come to Montgomery because "I just wanted to come down to be with you." The author James Baldwin, who was living in France but had returned to the United States for the week, said that the march marked "the beginning of the end of Negro enslavement."

Rallying the rain-soaked crowd—described by *The New York Times* as a "bedraggled band of Alabama Negroes and sympathizers"—Martin Luther King Jr. shouted, "What do we want?" The crowd's response: "Freedom! Now!" He told them that the next day they would be engaging in "the greatest march that has ever been made on a state capitol in the South." And he exhorted "every self-respecting Negro" to join in.

But it was King's wife, Coretta, who stole the show, despite her reluctance to speak even after Belafonte insisted that she do so. Later, she recalled how dark it was that night, except for the lighted stage, and how she and her husband had struggled hand-in-hand through the crowd to get to the makeshift stage before being lifted onto it.[81]

"I told our companions on the march," she wrote, "that this was in the area where I had grown up and spoke of how returning to Montgomery ten years after we first went there had very special meaning for me. Then I spoke directly to the women about what all this means for the future of our children." Then she read from Langston Hughes's powerful poem "Mother to Son": "Well, son, I'll tell you: / Life for me ain't been no crystal stair / It's had tacks in it / And splinters / And boards torn up / And places with no carpet on the floor / Bare / But all the time / I'se been a-climbin' on / And reachin' landin's / And turnin' corners / And sometimes goin' in the dark / Where there ain't been no light / So, boy, don't you turn back / Don't you set down on the steps / 'Cause you finds it's kinder hard / Don't you fall now / For I'se still goin', honey / I'se still climbin' / And life for me ain't been no crystal stair."

Some in the crowd, however, like the Episcopal seminarian Jonathan Daniels, thought that the festivities were bordering on a shameless publicity stunt. He said that, yes, the entertainers were "good" and some of them were even "thrilling." But during the show, he said, he felt "as if I were at a circus."[82]

A reporter covering the event asked comedian Elaine May what she thought. "The only real circus," she replied, "is the state of Alabama and George Wallace."

CHAPTER 11

Loving the Hell Out of Alabama

Waking up on the morning of March 25, 1965—on what would be the last day of the march—I saw immediately a mass of humanity streaming into the muddy field/campground behind the City of St. Jude.

Hundreds of federal troops stood guard over the crowd, estimated to be two to three thousand. Army helicopters clattered overhead. I grabbed a cup of coffee as the tents we had slept in were being taken down, and we prepared to join the rest of the marchers for a scheduled 8:30 a.m. departure.

Thousands more were arriving, coming mainly from Montgomery, where they had spent the night. A light rain fell.

Harry Belafonte's wife, Julie—a ballet dancer—began to line up the entertainers who had put on the spectacular show the night before. She had been told to move them to the head of the march. Seeing the original three hundred marchers wearing orange plastic jackets, however, she said that *they* were the real stars. "We can't march here [at the front]," she said, as she led the celebrities around behind.[83]

Also falling in behind the original three hundred "foot soldiers" who had marched every day since Sunday were Martin Luther King Jr., Ralph Bunche, Ralph D. Abernathy, the Reverend Fred L. Shuttlesworth, and other civil rights leaders. Behind them was the grandfather of Jimmie Lee Jackson, who had been killed by an Alabama state trooper in nearby Perry County and whose death had triggered the march. There, too, was the Reverend Orloff Miller, a friend of the Reverend James Reeb, who had been beaten to death by segregationists in Selma earlier in the month. And behind them were the rest of us, now numbering about ten thousand.

Califano, of the Defense Department, wrote in a report filed at 10:00 a.m. that marchers had been scheduled to step off at 9:00 a.m. but were running late "because of a lack of organization." He said the marchers were due to arrive at the capitol in Montgomery at around noon. Then, they would conduct a rally until 3:00 p.m. and attempt to send twenty marchers to meet Governor Wallace, if he would have them, and disperse between 3:30 and 4:30 p.m.

That there was a "lack of organization" was an understatement. The delay in setting out as scheduled was also due to mixed signals—or no signals at all—that had been received by the military. Army jeeps positioned at a roadblock, for instance, prevented King's car from entering the City of St. Jude. His traveling aide, Bernard Lee, told the soldiers that the march could not begin without King. Andrew Young jumped from the car to deliver the same message, imploring the sergeant in charge to allow the car to make a left turn. Bunche also intervened.

"I'm Dr. Bunche, undersecretary of the United Nations," he told the sergeant. "Sorry, sir," the sergeant replied. "This is not the United Nations. My orders are no left turn."

As King was getting out of the car to ask Lee what was wrong, a Montgomery police officer on a motorcycle arrived on the scene. "You danged fool," he said to the sergeant, pointing to King. "This is the man. Let him through!"[84]

Death threats against the civil rights leader, meanwhile, continued to come in. So several black ministers were told to wear the same blue suit King wore to confuse any would-be sniper.[85]

At 11:00 a.m., under sunny skies—more than two hours later than originally planned—some ten thousand marchers, led by King, moved out. At his side was his wife, Coretta, who later recalled that it was a "genuine love of justice" that drove the marchers on despite the risks. "A human torrent of brotherhood," she wrote, "engulfed the 'Cradle of the Confederacy.'"

I recall marching through the African American section of Montgomery—north along Oak Street—and seeing mothers, fathers, and children cheering from ramshackle houses, urging us on.

A seventeen-year-old student from Hudson High School in Selma, Charles Mauldin, shouted to the onlookers, "Come march with us! You can't make your witness standing on the corner. We're going downtown. There's nothing to be afraid of." And many of them did join us, swelling our numbers to around twenty-five thousand.

From Oak Street, we headed up Mobile Street—crossing Jefferson Davis Avenue, named after the leader of the Confederacy, which amused us to no end—into Montgomery's downtown business district. Then, at Court Square, where Rosa Parks had boarded a segregated bus on December 1, 1955, and refused to give up her seat to a white passenger, triggering a citywide boycott of Montgomery's public transportation system by its African American population, we turned east onto Dexter Avenue where we could now see the Baptist church by the same name where King had served as pastor from 1954 to 1960.

As we passed the church, the street widened as we approached the whitewashed state capitol—with Confederate flags waving above the dome—up a slight hill a block away. A line of Alabama state troopers stood between us and the capitol, where Dexter Avenue came to an end at Bainbridge Street. On the steps of the capitol, where Jefferson Davis was sworn in as president of the Confederacy in February 1861, a second line of troopers stood guard.

"This is a revolution," Andrew Young called out to us over the loudspeakers, "a revolution that won't fire a shot...We come to love the hell out of the state of Alabama."

Some of the entertainers who had appeared at the "Stars for Freedom" rally the night before—Harry Belafonte; Peter, Paul, and Mary; Joan Baez; Odetta; the Chad Mitchell Trio—led the crowd in folk songs and spirituals, including "Blowin' in the Wind," "Go Tell It on the Mountain," and "This Land Is Your Land."

Then the speeches began—Ralph Bunche, A. Philip Randolph, Ralph D. Abernathy, Fred L. Shuttlesworth, John Lewis, James Farmer, Amelia Boynton—and as they did, Coretta Scott King looked over at Rosa Parks and thought about the many years of struggle, beginning with the Montgomery bus boycott a decade earlier.

"I realized we had really come a long way from our start in the bus protest," she wrote years later, "when only a handful of people, relatively speaking, were involved—all black people who were fighting for their dignity and the right to sit down in a bus. Now ten years had passed. We had desegregated the buses; we had desegregated public transportation, interstate as well as intrastate. Our right to use public accommodations had been guaranteed. We had progressed toward school integration."

But most importantly, she said, the issue had gained national attention. "When I looked out over the big crowd," she wrote, "I saw many white people and church people. There were more church people involved than in any demonstration we had ever had, and I said to Martin later that it was perhaps the greatest witness by the church since the days of the early Christians. I still believe that."[86]

Finally, it was King's turn to speak and to bring the two-hour program—and the march—to an end.

"Last Sunday, more than eight thousand of us started on a mighty walk from Selma, Alabama," he began. "We have walked on meandering highways and rested our bodies on rocky byways...Some of literally slept in the mud. We have been drenched by rains. Our bodies are tired and our feet are somewhat sore.

"They told us we wouldn't get here," he continued. "And there were those who said that we would get here only over their dead bodies. But all the world today knows that we are here and we are standing before the forces of power in the state of Alabama saying, 'We ain't goin' let nobody turn us around.'"

King said that the Selma movement had become a shining moment in the conscience of man. "If the worst in American life lurked in its dark streets," he said, "the best of American instincts rose passionately from across the nation to overcome it. There never was a moment in American history more honorable and more inspiring than the pilgrimage of clergymen and laymen of every race and faith pouring into Selma to face danger at the side of its embattled Negroes."

He paid his "profound respects," in particular, to the white Americans who "cherish their democratic traditions over the ugly customs and privileges of generations and come forth boldly to join hands with us.

"So I stand before you this afternoon with the conviction that segregation is on its deathbed in Alabama," he said, "and the only thing uncertain about it is how costly the segregationists and Wallace will make the funeral."

He said that some were asking how long it would take to achieve freedom and justice for all people.

"How long? Not long, because no lie can live forever. How long? Not long, because you shall reap what you sow...How long? Not long, because the arc of the moral universe is long, but it bends toward justice."

CHAPTER 12

Too Many People Just Talking

Listening to Martin Luther King Jr.'s speech at the end of the Selma-to-Montgomery march—along with the rest of us—was Viola Liuzzo, a thirty-nine-year-old white mother of five, who had driven from her home in Detroit to participate in the march. "I want to be part of it," she told her husband before leaving.

Liuzzo had considered making the trip after watching television coverage of "Bloody Sunday." It took her a week, however, to make the decision to leave her family and head south. Once she did, she took off immediately, alone, in the family's powder blue 1963 Oldsmobile, telling her husband, Anthony, that there were "too many people who just stand around talking." She arrived in Selma on Friday, March 19, after three days on the road—a day before we arrived in the city after a five-day trek from Ripon, Wisconsin, by way of Washington, DC.

A student at Detroit's Wayne State University, Liuzzo had participated in a sympathy march for the Selma protestors on March 16. She had also joined other students to discuss "Bloody Sunday" and other events in Selma with the Reverend Malcolm Boyd, a chaplain at the school.

Boyd, an Episcopal priest who had worked in the South for several years seeking to ease tensions between the races, told Liuzzo and the others that some Wayne State students were planning to travel to Alabama to participate in the Selma-to-Montgomery march (although, in the end, they would not make the trip).

"He's made me do a lot of thinking," Liuzzo said later referring to Boyd, who in 1961 had protested segregation in the public transportation system in the South, riding interstate buses with dozens of other black and white civil rights activists as one of CORE's "Freedom Riders."

On the morning of March 19, Liuzzo pulled up at Brown Chapel in Selma and was met by two African American teenagers who identified themselves as civil rights workers and asked to borrow her car to pick up people arriving for the march at Montgomery's bus and train stations, as well as at Dannelly Field. Without any hesitation, she gave them the keys.

Later that day she returned to Brown Chapel, after having settled into a room that had been assigned to her across the street, to check on her car. There she met Leroy Moton, a nineteen-year-old SCLC volunteer from Selma who was in charge of moving people around Montgomery in rental cars or private vehicles that had been volunteered for that purpose. He assured Liuzzo that her car was safe, and she agreed to formally turn it over to him for the duration of the march. On Saturday, he drove her to the City of St. Jude. She spent the rest of the day running a first-aid station for the protestors.

Up early the next day, Liuzzo asked one of the St. Jude priests, Father Timothy Deasy, if he would accompany her to the top the church tower to take a look out over the city, and he agreed. But as she and Deasy reached the small room at the pinnacle of the tower, a strange feeling came over her, and she rushed out onto the street, where she had a full-blown panic attack. "Father," she said, "I have a feeling...something is going to happen today. Someone is going to get killed." After saying a prayer or two, she felt better and joined the march to downtown Montgomery.[87]

After the march, she returned to St. Jude to retrieve her car, which she had loaned to Moton, who arrived at the complex around 6:00 p.m. with a carload of passengers—one heading to the airport and others back to Selma.

Together, with Liuzzo behind the wheel, they drove west on US Highway 80, dropping off the passenger at Dannelly Field, and then they continued on to Selma, where they deposited the remaining four passengers.

After a quick bite to eat, they set off for Montgomery to pick up more marchers who were returning to Selma. At a traffic light near the Edmund Pettus Bridge, they were spotted by four Klansmen in a red-and-white Chevrolet Impala. Later, it would be revealed that they had spent the day looking for an opportunity to kill Martin Luther King Jr. But now, instead, they decided to attack Liuzzo and Moton to send a message to northern whites, southern blacks, and like-minded liberals.

Moton would later recall that after crossing the Edmund Pettus Bridge, Liuzzo spoke about how she hoped to become more involved in the civil rights movement when she returned to Detroit. It was dark, he said, and US Highway 80, where the marchers had walked proudly and under the protection of federal troops earlier in the week, was now deserted.

"Mrs. Liuzzo was singing ["We Shall Overcome"] and talking," Moton said later, "but I didn't say a word. I almost say to her, we better turn around and go back. But then I say to myself, she probably wouldn't do it anyhow."

About twenty miles east of Selma—now in Lowndes County—the pair noticed a car following them at some distance with its headlights on high beam. After a few minutes, it pulled up alongside Liuzzo's car at high speed. There was gunfire, and fourteen bullets shattered the glass on the driver's side, killing Liuzzo instantly and sending the car off the road into a ditch. "I'm one hell of a shot," one of the Klansmen was reported to have said. "That bitch and that bastard are dead and in hell."

But Moton had survived the attack, and after pretending to be dead, he ran out onto the highway and after awhile flagged down a flatbed truck full of marchers from Selma. "A woman's been killed," he told the driver, a young minister from Richmond, California. "She's been shot!"[88]

Liuzzo was the third civil rights activist who had been killed in Alabama in less than a month—after Jimmie Lee Jackson, who was shot by an Alabama state trooper in Marion, and the Reverend James Reeb, the Unitarian Universalist minister from Boston who was beaten to death by white segregationists in Selma.

The next day condolences poured in to the Liuzzo family from around the country. President Johnson telephoned them to express his and Mrs. Johnson's sorrow at their loss. Vice President Hubert Humphrey paid a personal visit to the Liuzzo home in Detroit. And the Reverend Malcolm Boyd told a reporter that Liuzzo epitomized a strong person in the movement "who didn't ask to be a leader."

"People like Mrs. Liuzzo make up the moral backbone of the movement," Boyd said. "They are committed to freedom that they are really ready to die for."

The Grand Wizard of the United Klans of America—Robert M. Shelton of Tuscaloosa, Alabama—was asked if he knew anything about Liuzzo's murder. "I don't have any knowledge of any participation in any acts of violence by any members of our organization," he said.[89]

But in May 1965, three of the four men who were in the car that had fired on Liuzzo and Moton that night—William Orville Eaton, Eugene Thomas, and Collie Leroy Wilkins Jr., all members of the KKK—were indicted on a state charge of murder and brought to trial. The fourth, Gary Thomas Rowe Jr., turned out to be an undercover FBI informant and was protected from prosecution. An all-white jury was unable to reach a decision on guilt or innocence, and a mistrial was declared. A second trial later that year ended with a verdict of not guilty. But in a subsequent federal trial, they were found guilty of conspiring to violate the civil rights of Liuzzo and were sentenced to ten years behind bars.

CHAPTER 13

A Heroic Christian Deed

After the Selma-to-Montgomery march, I returned to Ripon College to finish my studies. The Greyhound bus I caught after the march had ended in downtown Montgomery was packed with fellow marchers and headed north, passing through cities and towns that like most in America were feeling the impact of the march and its aftermath, even far away.

Local newspapers on Friday, March 26, were filled with extensive coverage of the final day of the march and of the slaying of Viola Liuzzo in their later editions.

Some newspaper reports were skeptical, if not downright dismissive, quoting Governor Wallace, for instance, as saying that the march had been a "prostitution of the lawful process"—even though it had been authorized by the federal government.

The *Birmingham Post-Herald*, for instance, which I picked up at the bus station in Birmingham during a brief stopover, said in a front-page story that the march had been a failure. It quoted Wallace as saying that it had cost $1 million—an apparent reference to expenditures by the federal government to protect the marchers—and that known communists were among the marchers.

Wallace said that the twenty-man delegation appointed to deliver a petition on voting rights to him, headed by the Reverend Joseph Lowery of Birmingham, included people who he said belonged to organizations "cited as subversive" by the House Un-American Activities Committee, as well as known felons and "some nonresidents." He said he would not be intimidated by people "who come up here in a mob."

But *The Courier-Journal* in Louisville, Kentucky, which I bought during a longer stop there, provided front-page coverage that was more favorable to the march, focusing on the fact that Wallace had refused to meet the Lowery-led delegation. An editorial called Wallace and his followers racist. "The march from Selma to Montgomery was risky," it said. "Was it worth it? Yes. It was an eloquent answer to those who believe that brutality can prevail against aroused conscience, and a living dramatization of the determination of those who are dedicated to a new day of justice in Alabama."

In Indianapolis—as the bus now closed in on my hometown of Chicago, and eventually Ripon—I bought a copy of *The Indianapolis Times*, which highlighted coverage of the Liuzzo murder. The paper called it a "race killing" by a "night rider." It also provided extensive coverage of King's speech on the steps of the Alabama state capitol.

The *Chicago Daily News* used its front page on March 26 to highlight President Johnson's pledge to defeat the Ku Klux Klan, following the arrest of four KKK members in connection with Liuzzo's death.

"They struck by night as they generally do," Johnson was quoted by the newspaper as saying, "for their purposes cannot cannot stand the light of day." He said his father had fought the KKK in Texas, and that he would continue to fight them because "I believe them to threaten the peace of every community where they exist." He urged members of the shadowy organization to "get out...now and return to a decent society—before it is too late."

Eventually, we all made it back to Ripon, one way or another. But it was not a happy homecoming for some of us. Chaplain Thompson, who had led our small band of "outside agitators" to Alabama, immediately began to receive hate mail from concerned local residents and was declared persona non grata at his church for about two years—even as he publicly touted what one would have thought were values strongly supported by the Christian church: nonviolence and pacifism.

Thompson told the local newspaper, *The Ripon Commonwealth-Press*, that we had participated in "history in the making."

"As long as long as there are places in the United States where these rights are denied, it is up to us as Americans to do something about it," he said. "We can send money, but there are times when our physical presence is needed."

For my part, I was welcomed back on campus by students and faculty who were curious about the trip. But little on campus had changed. No, I was not naive enough to believe that one trip to Selma could spark a full-blown revolution. Yet it was clear that that the lines were still as sharply drawn as they had been between the students who thought that racial problems in the South were none of our business and those who thought they were.

James R. Bowditch, of the English Department, said in an op-ed piece published in the school newspaper a month after we returned that the campus "seems to have decided that little of importance has happened or is happening in Alabama and across the nation.

"Perhaps if we sit tight, ignore the Medgar Everses, the Jimmie Lee Jacksons, the Reebs and Liuzzos, the bombings and the cross burnings (we are so isolated, you know)," he wrote, "the whole mess will disappear. If we can persuade ourselves that those who cause disturbance by trying to integrate a public restaurant, enter a white church, register as full citizens or march to call attention to systematic and deliberate injustice are merely rabble-rousing exhibitionists, then perhaps we can turn our attention to less painful matters. Above all, if we can convince ourselves that the true patriot is he who keeps his nose out of others' affairs, then perhaps we can really enjoy the coming spring. Perhaps."

I continued to speak out about the issue, explaining to anyone who would listen what it was like "down South" and making the best case I could for sending what money they could to support the ongoing work of organizations like SNCC—but more importantly, for sending human beings.

Others from the North, meanwhile, stayed in the South to continue their work "agitating" for justice—like Jonathan Myrick Daniels, the twenty-six-year-old Episcopal seminarian, who had come to Alabama as part of a delegation from the Episcopal Theological School (ETS) in Cambridge, Massachusetts.

After the march, Daniels and his fellow seminarian Judith Upham made their way back to Selma, thinking about the "danger," no doubt, that King had referred to when he had talked about what faced those white citizens who had come from other parts of the country to stand "at the side of its embattled Negroes." It was not until the next day, however, that they would learn—like the rest of us—about Viola Liuzzo's murder on US Highway 80.

Those who knew Daniels, and those who like him experienced life in Alabama in the 1960s, remember it as a frightening time. Dozens of civil rights activists—black and white—were killed by white segregationists throughout the South, and countless others were beaten or otherwise verbally and physically intimidated.

Even seasoned civil rights activists like Julian Bond, the longtime civil rights leader, said that for him and others, it was a "scary time," particularly for those working to register African Americans in Lowndes County. To African Americans, the county was known simply as "Bloody Lowndes."

But Bond, a cofounder of SNCC, which supported the work of Daniels and others throughout the South, told me that he also remembers the spring and summer of 1965 as a hopeful time, with the enactment, for instance, of the Voting Rights Act of 1965, signed into law by President Johnson on August 6.

The legislation—approved overwhelmingly by members of Congress who were shocked into action by the events in Selma—suspended literacy tests for prospective voters in twenty-six states, including Alabama; replaced local officials serving as voter registrars with federal examiners; and empowered the attorney general to take action against state and local authorities who imposed a poll tax on voters.

Before signing the bill, President Johnson met with civil rights leaders and others in the Oval Office at the White House, including John Lewis, the twenty-five-year-old chairman of SNCC, who had been beaten badly by Alabama state troopers at the foot of the Edmund Pettus Bridge in Selma on "Bloody Sunday" in early March.

Lewis later recalled that Johnson, his feet propped up on a chair and his hands folded behind his head, suddenly leaned forward and told him, "Now, John, you've got to go back and get those folks registered. You've got to go back and get those boys by the balls. Just like a bull gets on top of a cow. You've got to get 'em by the balls, and you've got to *squeeze*, squeeze 'em till they *hurt*."

Lewis said later that he had heard that Johnson enjoyed speaking in graphic, down-home terms, "but I wasn't quite prepared for all those bulls and balls."[90]

A less profane priority for Jonathan Daniels, meanwhile, was working with other like-minded clergy and laymen in Selma to break down the longstanding barriers between blacks and whites by, for example, integrating the city's only Episcopal church, St. Paul's.

He and other Episcopalians had come to Selma despite strong opposition from Alabama's Episcopal bishop, Charles C. J. Carpenter, who had made it clear that civil rights activists, especially Episcopalians, would not be welcome in his diocese.

"Civil disobedience," Carpenter said, "is just another name for lawlessness."[91]

Efforts to integrate St. Paul's were being spearheaded in the spring of 1965 by the Reverend John B. Morris, executive director of the Episcopal Society for Cultural and Racial Unity (ESCRU), whose members had arrived in the city en masse in response to Martin Luther King Jr.'s call for support.

Morris and the other Episcopalians, including Daniels, were probably not aware that the vestry at St. Paul's met in special session on March 11 to review its policy on race relations and had voted twelve to two to allow visiting Episcopal clergy to be seated at the rear of the church for services but to leave it up to the ushers to decide whether to seat other visitors.[92]

Shortly after arriving in Selma, Daniels and about two dozen other seminarians and clergy took their case directly to St. Paul's then-rector, the Reverend T. Frank Matthews, who, in an hour-long meeting with the group, defended the longstanding ban on blacks, arguing that church policy was church policy.

When Morris and the Reverend Malcolm Peabody, president of the ESCRU board of directors, led an interracial group to St. Paul's on March 14 (a week before the Selma-to-Montgomery march would begin), they were informed by the ushers that only clergy and white laypeople would be allowed to attend the Sunday service. So they left the church—disappointed but not surprised—after praying together for a few minutes at the front of the brownstone edifice.

Opposed to the ban on interracial worship were two prominent members of the church and of Selma's white establishment: Miller Childers, an attorney who would later be named judge of the Dallas County Court and the District Court of Dallas County, and Harry W. Gamble Jr., another lawyer whose grandfather had earlier served as rector of the church.

Childers and Gamble told me recently that they recall seeing Daniels among the group of Episcopalian protesters that had showed up at the church that Sunday. They said they were disgusted by what the ushers had done in turning them away.

The church vestry, according to Childers, had been meeting almost daily to discuss what to do in response to the widening civil rights protests that had been shaking up normal life in Selma since the beginning of the year. He said he was one of only two members of the vestry who initially voiced concern over the church's policy of ignoring the edict issued by the General Convention of the Episcopal Convention the previous October amending Canon 16, which prohibited the exclusion of worshippers on the basis of race, color, or ethnic origin.

Church records show that on March 19, the vestry—perhaps influenced by the negative media publicity that had begun to surround the refusal of the church to allow blacks to worship at St. Paul's—narrowly rejected a resolution directing the church to abide by the newly amended Canon 16. But on March 22—the day after the Selma-to-Montgomery march had begun—the vestry approved the resolution by eight to three, with one abstention, effectively ending the church's century-plus record of racial segregation.

It is likely that the vestry had also been influenced by the persistence of Daniels and the other Episcopalian protestors in calling for an end to the ban, which included a procession of about two hundred ESCRU members on March 20 from Brown Chapel to St. Paul's, led by the Reverend C. Kilmer Myers, the suffragan bishop of Michigan, who had branded the Episcopal Church a "racist, caste-ridden" institution. Refused entry, the group celebrated communion on a makeshift altar set up on the sidewalk and then left.

On the Sunday after the Selma-to-Montgomery march—March 28—Daniels and his fellow seminarian, Judith Upham, along with nine other whites and five blacks, were admitted to St. Paul's for the 11:00 a.m. service. They were seated in the front row, where they listened to Matthews speak on the "Ministry of Reconciliation" without ever mentioning race relations or the controversy within the church.[93]

Gamble told me he recalls Daniels being "very low key and cordial," and not challenging or "in-your-face."

As for Childers, he and his family had paid a heavy price for having supported a reversal of St. Paul's policy of racial discrimination. His children were taunted by other children at school, he said, and friends and acquaintances avoided eye contact on hearing of his stand on the issue at St. Paul's. Asked why he did what he did in opposing the ban on blacks, Childers said, "I thought it was the right thing to do."

In May, after two months in Selma, Daniels returned to the Episcopal Theological School (ETS) in Cambridge, Massachusetts, for final examinations and graduation. In early July, after a brief vacation, he returned to Selma, this time by car, writing later that "something had happened to me in Selma, which meant I had to come back. I could not stand by in benevolent dispassion any longer without compromising everything I know and love and value. The imperative was too clear, the stakes too high..."

In Selma, Daniels found lodging with Alice and Lonzy West and their family in the African American section of the city, across from Brown Chapel. He continued to work to fully integrate St. Paul's Episcopal Church. He sought to open channels of communication with the white community. He encouraged blacks to register to vote. And he involved himself in projects aimed at improving health care, housing, and other social services for blacks in Dallas County.[94]

But he became increasingly frustrated with what he saw as his inability to make significant progress in working with local whites on race relations, and with the relatively routine nature of the work. "It may be too much to say I'm beginning to despair of Selma," he told Judith Upham, who was now in St. Louis, "but at any rate I am not optimistic." So in mid-July, he decided to shift his work to neighboring Lowndes County, where SNCC was active in protesting racial discrimination and registering African Americans to vote.[95]

On August 13, while picketing whites-only businesses in the small Lowndes County town of Fort Deposit, Daniels and about two dozen other protesters were arrested and taken by truck to the county jail in Hayneville, where most of them, including Daniels, were held for six days.

Released on August 20, Daniels and three others—Father Richard F. Morrisroe, a white Roman Catholic priest from Chicago, and two young black girls—went immediately to a local grocery store to buy a soda. Standing in the doorway was Thomas L. Coleman, a part-time deputy sheriff, armed with a shotgun, who ordered them to leave, aiming his gun at one of the girls, sixteen-year-old Ruby Sales. Daniels pushed her to the ground, and when Coleman opened fire the young seminarian took the full blast of the weapon straight on and died instantly.

A second blast from Coleman's gun struck Morrisroe in the back as he ran from the scene pulling the other girl, Joyce Bailey, with him. After several months in the hospital, Morrisroe recovered and returned to work on behalf of social justice in the Chicago area.

The next day, Coleman turned himself in, but six weeks later he was acquitted by an all-white jury after only two hours of deliberation. He died at his home in Hayneville in 1997 at the age of 86.

On hearing the news of Daniels's death, Martin Luther King Jr. called his selfless defense of Ruby Sales in Hayneville "one of the most heroic Christian deeds of which I have heard in my entire ministry..."

The Very Reverend Samuel T. Lloyd III, former dean of the Washington National Cathedral and now priest-in-charge at Trinity Church in Boston, told me that Daniels, recognized as a martyr by the Episcopal Church in 1994, took a stand against racial injustice at a time when the church was, in his view, "sluggish" on civil rights. "He stood for what we hope the church stands for today," Lloyd said, "and he gave his life for it."

Rachel West, then nine years old, has said that what she remembers most about Daniels—"a part of our family" and of "every black family in Selma"—was his boyish smile. "His eyes were clear and steady," she wrote. He was friendly, she said. But most of all he was gentle. "I know there were times when he must have been frightened," she said, "but he never showed it."

She said that one day, when she was playing outside with her friends, her mother, Alice, called to her, crying. "Our friend is dead," she recalls her mother saying. "They killed Jonathan."

"I must have cried the whole night," Rachel wrote. "Of all the things that happened during that movement, nothing touched me as deeply as his death...He had died trying to make peace. I'm sure that if he had had a choice, he would have preferred to have lived awhile; he was a very young person. But I also think that he preferred to die for a cause.

"From that first day he walked in with his suitcase and little knapsack," she recalled, "it was like an old friend coming home. We children loved him...When Jonathan came to us, I knew for certain that there were really good white folks in this country, and with them on our side we would win our freedom."

Her mother, Alice, told me that Daniels was "like a member of the family"—even though her neighbors were at first distrustful of this young white seminarian from the North. But they soon grew to like him, she said, eventually considering him to be part of the African American community.

She said she is proud of having been active in the civil rights movement at an early age, and she considers her most important contribution to the civil rights movement housing and feeding many of the civil rights workers who came to Selma in the 1960s. She said that Daniels, who stayed with the West family for several months, was the most well-liked of what she called the "outside agitators" who boarded with her family in their five-bedroom, two-bathroom apartment, which was known as the Freedom Rights Home.

She recalled that Daniels would leave the family apartment early in the morning for civil rights work in Lowndes County and return late at night. On that fateful day in August 1965, she said, he hugged and kissed her before he left. She said he said a special prayer for the West family before walking out to his car. But he came back. "He hugged me again," she said, "and said, 'Goodbye, Mrs. West. Please hug and kiss your children for me when they wake up.'" It was the last time she saw him.

She said that the Episcopal Church flew her and her family to Keene, New Hampshire—Daniels's hometown—to attend his funeral. "I couldn't believe it," she said, "seeing Jon lying there in his casket. All the black people in Selma loved him so." One of her grandsons, she said, is named Jonathan Myrick West.

CHAPTER 14

Nonviolence Runs Out

In the days following Jonathan Myrick Daniels's murder, memorial services honoring the fallen Episcopal seminarian were held in cities across the United States, including St. Louis, Chicago, Atlanta, and Boston.

The Reverend Malcolm Boyd, a fellow civil rights activist who had befriended Daniels in Selma earlier that summer, said at a requiem mass at the Episcopal Church of the Atonement in Washington, DC, on Sunday, August 22, 1965—two days after Daniels was killed—that he was "the most alive young man in the church I have met..."

"Theologically, he knew what he was doing," said Boyd, who was the Episcopal Church's chaplain-at-large for colleges and universities, "and in the church...he was one person who was not afraid of getting involved."[96]

But the main religious service in Daniels's honor was held two days later in his hometown of Keene, New Hampshire, where more than a thousand mourners filed past his casket at St. James Episcopal Church on Monday, August 23, and another four hundred on the morning of August 24, prior to the 1:00 p.m. service.

After the service—attended by some eight hundred people—a small group of mourners gathered around his grave after internment at Monadnock View Cemetery, next to his father, and sang softly and with tears in their eyes "We Shall Overcome."

Prominent in the group was Stokely Carmichael, the charismatic SNCC field secretary, who later shared with Boyd—also in attendance—some notes that he had made on the program during the service that day.

"Jon was not a religious man," Carmichael wrote. "He lived a religious life. Jon did not die for us all. His life was taken from him. Jon lived for us all. Jon did not get his strength from rituals. He got his strength from people. From whence cometh my strength? My strength cometh not from the hills. My strength cometh from men like Jon. Jon was not a follower of Christ. He lived like Christ."[97]

The previous night, at a mass meeting of African American residents in Lowndes County, Carmichael had said that crying over Daniels's death was not for him. "We ain't going to resurrect Jon," he said. "We're going to resurrect ourselves."

Carmichael had also exhorted the crowd to action, saying that African Americans were more committed to change now than ever before. "We're going to tear this country up," he said. "We're going to build it back up, until it's a fit place for human beings."[98]

His friendship with Daniels, he said later, was forged earlier that month when they were arrested with some two dozen other civil rights workers in Fort Deposit, Alabama, while picketing local stores for equal job opportunities.

"I was a little uneasy even about the picket itself," Carmichael later wrote, "which would be...the first direct action not directly related to voting in the county. But, I thought, hey, a public demonstration in the middle of the day. The media will be there. What can happen?"

The demonstration, in fact, turned out to be shorter than planned because a group of thugs from the Ku Klux Klan had been waiting for them. "We were immediately surrounded by a mob larger than the demonstration," he said, adding that it was one time he was not sorry to be arrested. At the jail in Hayneville, he said, the guards were quick to single out Daniels and Father Richard F. Morrisroe—the only two whites among those who were arrested—for abuse.[99]

Initially, Carmichael said, he had opposed Daniels and other whites working in Lowndes County. "This was not because we had any formal policy of excluding them," he said. "We simply did not encourage them. At that time [in Lowndes County], it was really like operating behind enemy lines."

Ruby Sales, whose life Daniels saved by shielding her from the shotgun blast outside the grocery store in Hayneville on August 20, said that one reason for the hesitancy among some blacks to allow white activists to work in Lowndes County—a Klan stronghold—was that their presence would incite local whites to violence.

"I was very afraid of unleashing uncontrolled violence because of Lowndes County's history," Sales told an interviewer. "But ultimately it was decided that the movement was an open place and should provide an opportunity for anyone who wanted to come and struggle against racism to be a part of that struggle."[100]

Carmichael said later he had been devastated by Daniels's murder. "He'd been in Selma a while and would always seek me out for serious discussions whenever I was there," he recalled. "I appreciated his intelligence and seriousness. In this he was a little different from the usual white activists you met. He was somewhat more thoughtful and analytic. Tried to think things through, didn't trot out glib slogans but was looking for lasting solutions...He was shocked and pained by the racism, injustice, and poverty he was seeing...I thought Jon was an impressive guy, very responsible...But what I should have said [to him] very firmly was, please, stay the heck away from Lowndes."[101]

As a SNCC project director, and having known Daniels so well, Carmichael was asked to personally inform the young seminarian's parents of their son's death. So he flew to New York City to pick up his mother for the drive to Keene.

"I had never seen my son like that," his mother, Mabel, recalled. "Silent, grim, like a heavy, heavy weight was pressing on him. Even when his father died, that had really hit him, but this was different...[It was] the only time he ever asked me to go with him on movement business. He told me the young man was his friend."

She said that her son said nothing during the entire trip. "He didn't even play the [car] radio," she said. When they arrived in Keene, he and Daniels's parents went into another room in the house. "I believe Stokely was crying," his mother said. "He never told me what was said. The trip back in the car was just as silent. I do think this was the hardest thing my son ever had to do in the movement."

Others who knew Daniels also said that his death and the acquittal by an all-white jury of his white assassin, Thomas L. Coleman, had clearly traumatized Carmichael. "He became distrustful of practically all whites," wrote Jack Nelson, the veteran civil rights reporter for *The Los Angeles Times*. "I could see the changes in him, watching as he turned bitter and cynical, cursing his country and saying that democracy was a failure."[102]

It is unclear, however, to what extent Daniels's murder triggered—or contributed to—Carmichael's eventual rejection of nonviolence as a means of achieving racial justice.

His immediate reaction to the murder was to bring in ten of SNCC's most experienced field secretaries to Lowndes County to work on voter registration. "We want to show the people that we are not afraid of Lowndes County," he said, "and that they can't run us out." He said he wanted to see at least four thousand African Americans registered to vote—up from none in March—by the time the additional field secretaries left the county.[103]

Carmichael later wrote that after Daniels was murdered, African Americans in Alabama saw no other choice than to prepare to defend themselves, and so they did.

"Jon's murder grieved us," he wrote. "His wasn't the first death we'd experienced. But it was in some ways the closest to me as an organizer... But we couldn't let that stop the work. That's precisely what the killers intended. However, from then on, a little too late, the [SNCC] project staff took the strong position, nonnegotiable, that to allow whites in would be tantamount to inviting their deaths. That became our policy. And we armed ourselves...We made a mistake with Jonathan. One that I always remember with regret."[104]

The radicalization of the civil rights movement became clear less than a year later when, at a SNCC meeting near Nashville, Tennessee, in May 1966, Carmichael was elected its new leader, replacing John Lewis, a staunch advocate of nonviolence.

Earlier that year, several SNCC dissidents working in Atlanta with the Vine City Project under the leadership of Bill Ware had put forward a paper calling for severing all ties with white activists. It would become, in retrospect, the opening volley in a pivotal struggle among blacks over the control of SNCC and the future direction of the movement.[105]

"If we are to proceed toward liberation," the paper argued, "we must cut ourselves off from white people." It said that whites should only play a minor role at best in civil rights activities or political organizing among African Americans. "We must form our own institutions, credit unions, co-ops, political parties, write our own histories."[106]

Not surprisingly, the paper caused an uproar among some members of the SNCC leadership, and Carmichael was forced to defend white workers against criticism from within the organization, underscoring his relatively complicated views on interracial cooperation.[107]

But by June of that year, he had abandoned any hope he might have had of working toward racial integration (although he would maintain his commitment to forming biracial progressive coalitions whenever possible), pinning his hopes instead on achieving economic and political power for all African Americans.

"What had happened in Alabama is that we started building something, and we made whites irrelevant to everything we did," Carmichael said in a June 1966 interview published in the *Movement*, SNCC's monthly magazine, in which he outlined what he and his colleagues had done to create an all-black political party in Lowndes County—later a model for the Black Panther Party, which was launched in Oakland, California, at the end of the year. "When you talk about going for power, moral force and nonviolence become completely irrelevant. When you go for power, you go for it the way everyone in the country goes for it."

Carmichael went on to criticize white liberals for "cutting out" when the chips were down, leaving poor blacks holding the bag. "But if you didn't depend on them for anything," he said, "you could do anything you wanted to do."

Also in June, in a speech in Greenwood, Mississippi, Carmichael for the first time employed a phrase that would soon send shockwaves throughout the country and the world: "Black Power."

James T. Patterson, the historian, has dismissed "Black Power" as "a vague and combative slogan."[108] Others have argued that it may have been too brash and angry and lacked any underlying political objective or strategy. Many mainstream newspapers also said that it presaged further violence and racial segregation.

But Carmichael—an alumnus of the nonviolent civil rights movement who turned militant, reflecting the mood among many African Americans at the time—knew better, noting that at a meeting of several hundred supporters at Mount Moriah Baptist Church in Selma on the evening of November 7, 1966, for instance, the audience did not have to waste their time arguing over the meaning of Black Power. "They understood [it]," he said.[109]

For the rest of this life, until his death in 1998 in self-imposed exile in Guinea at the age of fifty-seven, Carmichael would argue that seizing political power and not depending on legal remedies or moral suasion was the only way that racial justice in the United States could be achieved.

Dan T. Carter, former president of the Southern Historical Association, has called the Selma-to-Montgomery march the "nova" of the civil rights movement—"a brilliant climax, which brought to a close the nonviolent struggle that reshaped the South."[110]

John Lewis, the civil rights leader and Democratic congressman from Georgia, agreed, adding that the signing by President Johnson of the Voting Rights Act of 1965, whose passage was spurred by the events in Selma and the subsequent march to Montgomery, was the "last act" for the civil rights movement as he knew it.

"Something was born in Selma during the course of that year," Lewis has said. "But something died there, too. The road of nonviolence had essentially run out...It had been Selma that held us together as long as we did. After that, we [as a movement] just came apart."[111]

EPILOGUE

I did not recognize him at first—this elderly, bearded, black man standing in the back of the room with his clenched fist punching the sky, shouting "Black Power!" "Black Power!" "Black Power!"

Curious, I asked the man sitting next to me who he was. That's Mukasa Dada, he replied. Who? Maybe you know him, he said, as Willie Ricks.

Indeed I did. It was difficult, in fact, not to have known him in the mid-1960s when I ventured south to join the civil rights movement. He was everywhere, stirring up trouble.

An associate of Stokely Carmichael, Ricks was one of the most charismatic and effective organizers that the movement had ever known: the brains and brawn behind countless sit-ins, marches, demonstrations, and boycotts throughout the South. And it was Ricks, one of the most militant members of the Student Nonviolent Coordinating Committee (SNCC), who thrust "Black Power" into the forefront of the consciousness of many African Americans—not only in the South but across the country.

Martin Luther King Jr. has said (in *Where Do We Go from Here: Chaos or Community?* published in 1968) that it was Ricks, "the fiery orator of SNCC," who urged Carmichael to use "Black Power" as a movement slogan for the first time at an outdoor rally in Greenwood, Mississippi, in June 1966.

King said that at the rally, Carmichael mounted the platform and after arousing the audience with a powerful attack on Mississippi justice shouted, "What we need is black power." Then, Ricks leaped to the platform and shouted to the crowd, "What do you want?" And the crowd roared, "Black Power!" Again and again, according to King, Ricks cried, "What do you want?" and the response "Black Power" grew louder and louder, until it reached a fever pitch.

According to Carmichael, who has often been (inaccurately) credited with (or blamed for) introducing the phrase, the notion of black power was nothing new. "We'd been talking about nothing else in the Delta for years," he wrote. "The only difference was that this time [in Greenwood, Mississippi] the national media were there...As I passed [Ricks], he said, 'Drop it now. The people are ready. Drop it now.'"

The phrase, in fact, had been around for years. Richard Wright had used it for the title of his book on African politics, published in 1954. The African American singer, actor, and activist Paul Robeson used it, too. And Harlem politician Adam Clayton Powell Jr. had also employed it, telling students at Howard University in a May 1966 baccalaureate address, for instance, "to demand these God-given rights is to seek black power."

But it was Ricks, a twenty-three-year-old SNCC field secretary at the time, who pushed "Black Power!" as a slogan to replace King's "Freedom Now!" nearly fifty years ago.

Now seventy years old, Ricks told me he joined the struggle for racial justice as a high school student in Chattanooga, Tennessee, and grew increasingly militant following the murder of a close friend during a civil rights protest and was soon calling himself a black nationalist and supporting armed self-defense for his fellow African Americans. His attitude toward whites has been described as hostile.

A reporter for *The New York Times,* Roy Reed, who knew Ricks on a first-name basis in the 1960s, has recalled that Ricks told him one day there would be revolution in the United States and, in fact, it was already under way. It would lead to the deaths of many white people, he said. Then, looking the reporter straight in the eyes, he said, "When the revolution gets here, and if I ever see you in the sights of my gun, I'll pull the trigger." Reed said (in his memoir *Beware of Limbo Dancers: A Correspondent's Adventures with the New York Times,* published in 2012) that he knew deep down that Ricks was serious.

Now, some fifty years later, after decades of being beaten, jailed, bitten by dogs, and shot at, here he was in the audience at a seminar in a college auditorium in Selma, Alabama, still making noise and committed to the cause.

After the seminar, I asked him how he feels about whites today. He said he has never had anything against individual white people, and that his motivation for supporting the expulsion of whites from SNCC was rooted in the belief that the struggle for black rights needed to be led by blacks and that white liberals should organize poor whites and fight racism in their own communities.

The next day, Ricks told me he still believes that blacks need to create their own future. He said he admires Martin Luther King Jr.—"a servant of the people"—but, along with Carmichael and others, he had had a fundamental disagreement with him over the need for interracial cooperation.

King has said that, in his view, "Black Power" was an "unfortunate choice of words." He said that after Carmichael and Ricks had spoken to the crowd in Greenwood, Mississippi, he asked them—along with Floyd McKissick, the leader of the Congress of Racial Equality (CORE)—to meet with him to discuss the issue. For five hours, he said, he pleaded with them to abandon the "Black Power" slogan.

"It was my contention that a leader has to be concerned about the problem of semantics," King said. "The slogan 'Black Power' carried the wrong connotations...I conceded the fact that we must have slogans. But why have one that would confuse our allies, isolate the Negro community and give many prejudiced whites, who might otherwise be ashamed of their anti-Negro feeling, a ready excuse for self-justification?" He said that the words "black" and "power" together give the impression that the issue being talked about is black domination rather than black equality.

King said that behind the "Black Power" slogan's "legitimate and necessary concern for group unity and black identity" lies the belief that there can be a separate black road to power and fulfillment. "Few ideas are more unrealistic," he said. "There is no salvation for the Negro through isolation...In a multiracial society no group can make it alone."

But Carmichael and McKissick were adamant, arguing that King's proposal to use "Black Consciousness" or "Black Equality" as slogans lacked the "ready appeal and persuasive force" of "Black Power." The meeting ended with the staff members of King's Southern Christian Leadership Conference (SCLC) agreeing that the "Black Power" slogan was unfortunate and would only divert attention from the evils of racism and with the staff members of CORE and SNCC insisting that it should be spread nationwide.

And indeed it was, with Carmichael exploiting his strident rhetoric and evolving black power philosophy to oust John Lewis—a civil rights pioneer, cofounder of SNCC, and staunch advocate of nonviolence—as the chairman of the organization. Its new objective, he said in an interview with SNCC's monthly magazine *The Movement* in June 1966, was to make whites "irrelevant to everything we did." In the interview, he also outlined what he and his colleagues had done to create an all-black political party in Alabama's Lowndes County, which would later become a model for the Black Panther Party, launched in Oakland, California, at the end of the year.

"When you talk about going for power, moral force and nonviolence become completely irrelevant," Carmichael said. "When you go for power, you go for it the way everyone in the country goes for it."

The distinguished African American historian Clayborne Carson, who is director of the Martin Luther King Jr. Research and Education Institute, has said that Carmichael's popularization of black power opened a new chapter in the transformation of the political consciousness of African Americans, particularly among those—mainly in the urban centers of the North—whose hopes were raised by the nonviolent civil rights struggle but not fulfilled.

"It was during the year of Carmichael's chairmanship that SNCC acquired unprecedented importance as a source of new political ideas,"

Carson wrote. "SNCC did not itself change the direction of black politics, but it did reflect a shift in the focus of black struggles from the rural South to the urban North and from civil rights reforms to complex, interrelated problems of poverty, powerlessness and cultural subordination... Millions of black people were prepared to adopt the rhetoric of black power in order to express their accumulated anger and to assume new, more satisfying racial identities."

For the rest of this life, in fact, Carmichael would argue that seizing political power—and not depending on legal remedies or moral suasion—was the only realistic path to racial justice in the United States.

Yet internal divisions within SNCC and the rise in racial violence hampered the ability of the organization, according to Carson, to transform black discontent into programs for achieving black power.

"[A]s it became more isolated from former white allies and more openly identified with uncontrollable urban black militancy," Carson wrote, "[SNCC] encountered ruthless government repression [and] their message would reach an ever-decreasing number of blacks."

As for Willie Ricks, who lives in Atlanta, he can still be found upholding his reputation as the "fiery orator," firing up crowds with revolutionary rhetoric at events honoring Martin Luther King Jr. Or at reunions of the Black Panther Party. Or celebrating the birth of the New Black Panther Party. Or attempting to organize students at Morehouse College in Atlanta (King's alma mater) but instead suffering a beating at the hands of the campus police, he says, for "trespassing." But always raising his clenched fist and shouting "Black Power!" "Black Power!" "Black Power!"

BIBLIOGRAPHY

Bass, S. Jonathan. *Blessed Are the Peacemakers: Martin Luther King, Jr., Eight White Religious Leaders and the "Letter from Birmingham Jail."* Baton Rouge: Louisiana State University Press, 2001.

Belafonte, Harry. *My Song: A Memoir.* New York: Alfred A. Knopf, 2011.

Belfrage, Sally. *Freedom Summer.* New York: The Viking Press, 1965.

Boyd, Malcolm. *As I Live and Breathe: Stages of an Autobiography.* New York: Random House, Inc. 1965.

Branch, Taylor. *At Canaan's Edge: America in the King Years 1965–68.* New York: Simon & Schuster, 2006.

———. *Parting the Waters: American in the King Years 1954–1963.* New York: Simon & Schuster, 1988.

———. *Pillar of Fire: America in the King Years 1963–65.* New York: Simon & Schuster, 1998.

Bruns, Roger. *Jesse Jackson: A Biography.* Westport, CT: Greenwood Press, 2005.

Carmichael, Stokely (with Ekwueme Michael Thelwell). *Ready for Revolution: The Life and Struggles of Stokely Carmichael.* New York: Scribner, 2003.

Carpenter, Douglas M. *A Powerful Blessing: The Life of Charles Colcock Jones Carpenter, Sr.* Birmingham, AL: TransAmerica Printing, 2012.

Carson, Clayborne. *In Struggle: SNCC and the Black Awakening of the 1960s.* Cambridge, MA: Harvard University Press, 1981.

Carter, Dan T. *The Politics of Rage: George Wallace, the Origins of the New Conservatism, and the Transformation of American Politics.* New York: Simon & Schuster, 1995.

Curry, Constance. *Deep in Our Hearts: Nine White Women in the Freedom Movement.* Athens, GA: University of Georgia Press, 2000.

Eagles, Charles W. *Outside Agitator: Jon Daniels and the Civil Rights Movement in Alabama.* Tuscaloosa, AL: University of Alabama Press, 2000.

Edelman, Marian Wright. *Lanterns: A Memoir of Mentors.* Boston: Beacon Press, 1999.

Fager, Charles E. *Selma, 1965.* New York: Charles Scribner's Sons, 1974.

Forman, James. *The Making of Black Revolutionaries.* New York: The Macmillan Company, 1972.

Friedland, Michael B. *Lift Up Your Voice Like a Trumpet: White Clergy and the Civil Rights and Antiwar Movements, 1954–1973.* Chapel Hill, NC: University of North Carolina Press, 1998.

Garrow, David J. *Protest at Selma: Martin Luther King, Jr., and the Voting Rights Act of 1965.* New Haven, CT: Yale University Press, 1978.

BIBLIOGRAPHY

Hampton, Henry, and Fayer, Steve. *Voices of Freedom: An Oral History of the Civil Rights Movement From the 1950s through the 1980s.* New York: Bantam Books, 1990.

Hill, Lance. *The Deacons for Defense: Armed Resistance and the Civil Rights Movement.* Chapel Hill, NC: University of North Carolina Press, 2004.

Howlett, Duncan. *No Greater Love: The James Reeb Story.* Boston: Skinner House Books, 1993.

Jeffries, Hasan Kwame. *Bloody Lowndes: Civil Rights and Black Power in Alabama's Black Belt.* New York: New York University Press, 2009.

Jenkins, Carol, and Hines, Elizabeth Gardiner. *Black Titan: A. G. Gaston and the Making of a Black American Millionaire.* New York: Random House Publishing Group, 2004.

Joseph, Peniel E. *Dark Days, Bright Nights: From Black Power to Barack Obama.* Philadelphia: Basic Civitas Books, 2010.

Katagiri, Yasuhiro. *The Mississippi State Sovereignty Commission: Civil Rights and States' Rights.* Jackson, MS: University Press of Mississippi, 2001.

Kennan, George F. *Sketches from a Life.* New York: Pantheon Books, 1989.

King, Coretta Scott. *My Life with Martin Luther King, Jr.* New York: Holt, Rinehart and Winston, 1969.

King, Martin Luther, Jr. *Where Do We Go from Here: Chaos or Community?* Boston: Beacon Press, 1968.

Lewis, John. *Walking with the Wind: A Memoir of the Movement.* New York: Harcourt Brace & Company, 1998.

Longenecker, Stephen L. *Selma's Peacemaker: Ralph Smeltzer and Civil Rights Mediation.* Philadelphia: Temple University Press, 1987.

May, Gary. *The Informant: The FBI, the Ku Klux Klan and the Murder of Viola Liuzzo.* New Haven, CT: Yale University Press, 2005.

McGuire, Danielle L. *At the Dark End of the Street: Black Women, Rape, and Resistance—a New History of the Civil Rights Movement from Rosa Parks to the Rise of Black Power.* New York: Alfred A. Knopf, 2010.

Mendelsohn, Jack. *The Martyrs: 16 Who Gave Their Lives for Racial Justice.* New York: Harper & Row, 1966.

Moore, Paul. *Presences: A Bishop's Life in the City.* New York: Farrar, Straus and Giroux, 1997.

Nelson, Jack. *Scoop: The Evolution of a Southern Reporter.* Jackson, MS: University of Mississippi Press, 2013.

Patterson, James T. *The Eve of Destruction: How 1965 Transformed America.* New York: Basic Books, 2012.

Payne, Charles M. *I've Got the Light of Freedom: The Organizing Tradition and the Mississippi Freedom Struggle.* Berkeley, CA: University of California Press, 1995.

Priestley, Justine. *By Gertrude Wilson: Dispatches of the 1960s, From a White Writer in a Black World.* Edgartown, MA: Vineyard Stories, 2005.

Raines, Howell. *My Soul Is Rested.* New York: G. P. Putnam's Sons, 1977.

Reed, Roy. *Beware of Limbo Dancers: A Correspondent's Adventures with the New York Times.* Fayetteville, AR: University of Arkansas Press, 2012.

Rice, Condoleezza. *Extraordinary, Ordinary People: A Memoir of Family.* New York: Crown Archetype, 2010.

Roberts, Gene, and Klibanoff, Hank. *The Race Beat: The Press, the Civil Rights Struggle, and the Awakening of a Nation.* New York: Alfred A. Knopf, 2006.

Shattuck, Gardiner H., Jr. *Episcopalians and Race: Civil War to Civil Rights.* Lexington, KY: University Press of Kentucky, 2000.

Washington, James Melvin, ed. *A Testament of Hope: The Essential Writings of Martin Luther King, Jr.* San Francisco: Harper and Row, 1986.

Watson, Bruce. *Freedom Summer: The Savage Season That Made Mississippi Burn and Made America a Democracy.* New York: Viking Penguin, 2010.

Williams, Juan. *Eyes on the Prize: America's Civil Rights Years, 1954–1965.* New York: Viking Penguin Inc., 1987.

Wilford, Hugh. *The Mighty Wurlitzer: How the CIA Played America.* Cambridge, MA: Harvard University Press, 2008.

Young, Andrew. *An Easy Burden: The Civil Rights Movement and the Transformation of America.* New York: HarperCollins Publishers, Inc., 1996.

Zellner, Bob. *The Wrong Side of Murder Creek: A White Southerner in the Freedom Movement.* Montgomery, AL: NewSouth Books, 2008.

INDEX

Abernathy, Ralph D. 35, 53, 73, 87, 90

Adler, Renata 39

Aelony, Zev 57

Alexander, William 20

Allen, Lewis 64, 65

Ashley, Robert 22, 23, 25

Baez, Joan 89

Bailey, Joyce 105

Baker, Wilson 8, 9, 45

Baldwin, James 35, 77, 85

Beittel, Adam D. 19

Belafonte, Harry 35, 77-85, 87, 89

Bennett, Tony 77, 84

Bernstein, Leonard 77, 84, 85

Bevel, James 18, 29

Blackwell, Randolph T. 3

Blue, Willie 80, 81

Bond, Julian 65, 100

Bowditch, James R. 99

Boyd, Malcolm 93, 96, 107

Boynton, Amelia 1, 2, 90

Braden, Anne 57, 62

Califano, Joseph A. 40, 41, 43, 52, 67, 88

Carmichael, Stokely 43, 107-112, 115, 116, 118, 119

Carota, Noel 29, 33

Carpenter, Charles C. J. 4, 36, 48-50, 101

Carson, Clayborne 118, 119

Carter, Dan T. 112

Caston, E. L. 64

Chaney, James viii, 57, 61, 78, 80

Childs, Miller 102, 103

Clark, Jim viii, 2, 10, 13, 30, 45, 73

Coleman, Thomas L. 104, 105, 110

Collins, LeRoy 43

Crowley, John 74, 75

Curry, Constance 57

Daniels, Jonathan Myrick 4-8, 36, 47, 48, 85, 100-110

Darin, Bobby 77

Davis, Ossie 77

Davis, Sammy 77, 84

Deasy, Timothy 94

De Lissovoy, Peter 57

Dickinson, William L. 72

Dinkins, William 8

Doar, John M. 52

Eaton, William Orville 96

Ellerbrake, Richard P. 58-60

Ellington, Duke 78

Evans, Roland 43, 44

Evers, Medgar 84

Fager, Charles E. 84

Falwell, Jerry 69

Farmer, James viii, 90

Fischer, Tom 24

Forman, James 7, 33, 34, 78-80

Fuson, Harold 45

Galligan, Eymard 74, 75

Gamble, Harry W. 102, 103

Gaston, A. G. 53, 54, 67

Glaser, John F. 16

Goodman, Andrew viiim 57, 61, 78, 80

Goodson, W. Kenneth 31

Gregory, Dick 29, 84

Grimsrud, Dick 14, 18-20, 28, 33, 34

Hall, David 37

Hall, Harris T. 28

Hanes, Art 30

Hanna, Mark 28

Hansen, Bill 57

Harris, David L. 25

Harris, Ella Holladay 73

Hayden, Casey 57, 61, 63, 64, 69-71

Hayden, Tom 70

Hayes, Kenneth 20

Heinz, Chris 51

Herbers, John 42

Heschel, Abraham 35

Hess, Jim 19

Hines, John E. 4, 11, 47

Hodierne, Robert 44, 45

Hunt, Patrick 21

Hurst, E. H. 64, 65

Iakovos, Archbishop 11

Jackson, Jesse L. 4

Jackson, Jimmie Lee viii, 87, 95, 99

Jackson, Sullivan 5, 7, 12, 35

Johnson, Frank M. 12

Johnson, Lyndon B. ix, 7, 9-13, 21, 26, 27, 30, 43, 73, 84, 96, 98, 100-102

Jones, Albert 58, 59

Jones, Daniel 65

Kennan, George F. 15-17

Kerlin, George 51

King, A. D. 41

King, Alan 77

King, Coretta Scott 11, 43, 78, 85, 88, 90

King, Martin Luther vii, viii, 1, 3-7, 11, 12, 17, 18, 29, 31, 33-35, 37, 39, 41-44, 47, 49, 50, 52-55, 68, 71-73, 75, 78, 84, 85, 87-90, 93, 95, 98, 100, 101, 105, 115-119

King, Mary E. 61

Kupcinet, Irv 79

Lee, Herbert 64, 65

Lee, Bernard 88

Lewis, John vii, 1, 2, 12, 29, 35, 37, 43, 44, 63, 70, 83, 90, 101, 111-113, 118

Leonard, Richard D. 69

Liuzzo, Viola 93-96

Lloyd, Samuel T. 105

Lowenstein, Allard K. 62, 63

Lowery, Joseph 97

Matthews, T. Frank 47, 48, 52, 102, 103

Mauldin, Charles 89

May, Elaine 77, 84, 86

McCarthy, Joseph 16, 27

McDonald, Howard 59

McGuire, Danielle L. 72

McKissick, Floyd 117, 118

Meadows, A. R. 68

Mettling, Carla 19, 20

Miller, Orloff 7, 87

Miller, Dotty 57

Mitchell, Chad 84, 89

Montgomery, Paul 39, 40

Moore, Paul 9, 27, 28

Moore, William L. 57

Morris, John B. 48, 101

Morrisroe, Richard F. 104, 105, 108

Moses, Bob 62, 63, 65, 66

Moton, Leroy 94-96

Mullaney, Paul J. 74

Myers, C. Kilmer 48, 50, 51, 103

Nabrit, James M. 12

Nash, Diane 7

Nelson, Jack 110

Nichols, Mike 77, 84

Novak, Robert 43, 44

Odetta 84, 89

Olsen, Clark 7, 8

Orris, Peter 65

Ouellet, Maurice 51, 74, 75

Parks, Rosa 14, 72, 89, 90

Patterson, Floyd 77

Patterson, James T. 112

Pate, Russell 31

Peabody, Malcolm 48, 102

Perdew, John 57

Perkins, Tony 77

Peter, Paul, and Mary 77, 89

Phillips, John F. 45

Pickard, J. A. 68

Pinkham, Fred O. 14

Poitier, Sidney 79-81

Powell, Adam Clayton 116

Proxmire, William 27

Purks, Jim 41

Quave, Laz 59

Race, John A. 27

Randolph, A. Phillip 35, 90

Reeb, James viii, 6-11, 26, 35, 87, 95, 99

Reed, James E. 24

Reed, Roy 23, 40, 42, 116

Reuther, Walter 11

Ricks, Willie 115-117, 119

Robeson, Paul 79

Robinson, Plater 65

Rowe, Gary Thomas 96

Rueger, Fred 24

Russell, Nipsey 84

Ryals, Frank 43

Sales, Ruby 104, 105, 109

Samuel, Morris V. 47

Schulke, Flip 39

Schwarz, David 20, 21, 23

Schwerner, Michael viii, 57, 61, 78, 80

Shelton, Robert M. 33, 96

Sherrod, Charles 61

Shirah, Sam 57

Shuttlesworth, Fred L. 87, 90

Simone, Nina 77, 84

Singer, Richard 23

Sitton, Claude 40

Smeltzer, Ralph E. 51, 52

Smitherman, Joe T. 8, 10, 30, 37, 68

Steele, Rosie 43

Stockstill, Jesse E. 59, 60

Thomas, Eugene 96

Thompson, Jerry vii, ix, 14, 18-23, 26, 28, 33, 98, 99

Toolen, Thomas J. 51, 74, 75,

INDEX

Tynes, Morris H. 71

Upham, Judith 36, 100, 103, 104

Van Hengel, Jean 25

Wallace, George C. 9, 18, 27, 29, 30, 51, 72, 73, 84, 86, 91, 97, 98

Ware, Bill 111

Watkins, Hollis 61

West, Alice 104, 106

West, Lonzy 104

West, Rachel 105

Wilhelm, Henry 44

Wilkes, Larry 24

Wilkins, Collie Leroy 96

Williams, Hosea 1, 5

Winters, Shelley 77, 84

Wolf, John 44

Woodman, Jerry 73

Wright, Richard 116

Young, Andrew 1, 3, 5, 29, 34, 52, 88, 89

Zellner, Bob 57, 61, 64, 70

NOTES

[1]   John Lewis, *Walking with the Wind: A Memoir of the Movement* (New York: Harcourt Brace & Company, 1998), pp. 340–341.

[2]   Juan Williams, *Eyes on the Prize: America's Civil Rights Years, 1954–1965* (New York: Viking Penguin Inc., 1987), p. 269.

[3]   Lewis, *Walking with the Wind: A Memoir of the Movement*, p. 344.

[4]   Ibid., p. 345.

[5]   *Selma-Times Journal*, March 8, 1965.

[6]   Taylor Branch, *At Canaan's Edge: America in the King Years 1965–68* (New York: Simon & Schuster, 2006), p. 45.

[7]   Michael B. Friedland, *Lift Up Your Voice Like a Trumpet: White Clergy and the Civil Rights and Antiwar Movements, 1954–1973* (Chapel Hill, NC: University of North Carolina Press, 1998), p. 122.

[8]   Charles E. Fager, *Selma, 1965* (New York: Charles Scribner's Sons, 1974), p. 97.

[9]   Friedland, *Lift Up Your Voice Like a Trumpet: White Clergy and the Civil Rights and Antiwar Movements, 1954–1973*, p. 122.

[10]   Gardiner H. Shattuck Jr., *Episcopalians and Race: Civil War to Civil Rights* (Lexington, KY: University Press of Kentucky, 2000), p. 154.

[11]   Roger Bruns, *Jesse Jackson: A Biography* (Westport, CT: Greenwood Press, 2005), p. 31.

[12]   Charles W. Eagles, *Outside Agitator: Jon Daniels and the Civil Rights Movement in Alabama* (Tuscaloosa, AL:

University of Alabama Press, 2000), p. 27.

13   Ibid., pp. 34–35.

14   Branch, *At Canaan's Edge: America in the King Years 1965–68*, p. 64.

15   Ibid., pp. 71–73.

16   Duncan Howlett, *No Greater Love: The James Reeb Story* (Boston: Skinner House Books, 1993), pp. 193*ff.*

17   Branch, *At Canaan's Edge: America in the King Years 1965–68*, pp. 75–76.

18   Ibid., p. 79.

19   Howlett, *No Greater Love: The James Reeb Story*, pp. 208*ff.*

20   *Selma Times-Journal*, March 10, 1965.

21   Ibid.

22   Fager, *Selma, 1965*, pp. 116*ff.*

23   Paul Moore, *Presences: A Bishop's Life in the City* (New York: Farrar, Straus and Giroux, 1997), p. 184.

24   David J. Garrow, *Protest at Selma: Martin Luther King, Jr., and the Voting Rights Act of 1965* (New Haven, CT: Yale University Press, 1978), pp. 100–101.

25   Ibid., p. 102.

26   Coretta Scott King, *My Life with Martin Luther King, Jr.* (New York: Holt, Rinehart and Winston, 1969), p. 263.

27   Branch, *At Canaan's Edge: America in the King Years 1965–68*, pp. 101–108.

28   Lewis, *Walking with the Wind: A Memoir of the Movement*, pp. 353–354.

29   George F. Kennan, *Sketches from a Life* (New York: Pantheon Books, 1989), pp. 205*ff.*

30   Taylor Branch, *Pillar of Fire: America in the King Years 1963–65* (New York: Simon & Schuster, 1998), p. 599.

31   Paul Moore, *Presences: A Bishop's Life in the City* (New

York: Farrar, Straus and Giroux, 1997), p. 183.

[32] Lewis, *Walking with the Wind: A Memoir of the Movement*, p. 357.

[33] Ibid., p. 356.

[34] Stokely Carmichael (with Ekwueme Michael Thelwell), *Ready for Revolution: The Life and Struggles of Stokely Carmichael* (New York: Scribner, 2003), p. 445.

[35] Branch, *At Canaan's Edge: America in the King Years 1965–68*, p. 141.

[36] Lewis, *Walking with the Wind: A Memoir of the Movement*, p. 358*ff.*

[37] Williams, *Eyes on the Prize: America's Civil Rights Years, 1954–1965*, p. 282.

[38] Gene Roberts and Hank Klibanoff, *The Race Beat: The Press, the Civil Rights Struggle, and the Awakening of a Nation* (New York: Alfred A. Knopf, 2006), p. 383.

[39] Ibid., p. 389.

[40] *The New York Times*, March 22, 1965.

[41] Roberts and Klibanoff, *The Race Beat: The Press, the Civil Rights Struggle, and the Awakening of a Nation*, p. 349.

[42] Ibid., p. 378.

[43] King, *My Life with Martin Luther King, Jr.*, p. 247.

[44] *The Selma Times-Journal*, March 23, 1965.

[45] *The Washington Post*, March 18, 1965.

[46] Charles W. Eagles, *Outside Agitator: Jon Daniels and the Civil Rights Movement in Alabama* (Tuscaloosa, AL: University of Alabama Press, 2000), p. 41.

[47] Gardiner H. Shattuck Jr., *Episcopalians and Race: Civil War to Civil Rights* (Lexington, KY: University Press of Kentucky, 2000), p. 155.

[48] Friedland, *Lift Up Your Voice Like a Trumpet: White Clergy and the Civil Rights and Antiwar Movements, 1954–1973*, p.

114.

[49]   Ibid., p. 116.

[50]   *The Selma-Times Journal,* February 2, 1965.

[51]   *The New York Times,* March 24, 1965.

[52]   Richard D. Leonard, *Call to Selma: Eighteen Days of Witness* (Boston: Skinner House Books, 2002), p. 104.

[53]   *The New York Times,* March 24, 1965.

[54]   Branch, *At Canaan's Edge: America in the King Years 1965–68,* pp. 152–153.

[55]   *Cleveland Plain Dealer,* March 24,1965.

[56]   Charles M. Payne, *I've Got the Light of Freedom: The Organizing Tradition and the Mississippi Freedom Struggle* (Berkeley, CA: University of California Press, 1995), p. 34.

[57]   Clayborne Carson, *In Struggle: SNCC and the Black Awakening of the 1960s* (Cambridge, MA: Harvard University Press, 1981), p. 67.

[58]   Ibid., p. 70.

[59]   Henry Hampton and Steve Fayer, *Voices of Freedom: An Oral History of the Civil Rights Movement from the 1950s through the 1980s* (New York: Bantam Books, 1990), p. 183.

[60]   Carson, *In Struggle: SNCC and the Black Awakening of the 1960s,* p. 99.

[61]   Ibid., p. 76.

[62]   Hampton and Fayer, *Voices of Freedom: An Oral History of the Civil Rights Movement from the 1950s through the 1980s,* pp. 185–186.

[63]   Ibid., pp. 184–185.

[64]   Bob Zellner, *The Wrong Side of Murder Creek: A White Southerner in the Freedom Movement* (Montgomery, AL: NewSouth Books, 2008), p. 246.

[65]   Hampton and Fayer, *Voices of Freedom: An Oral History of the Civil Rights Movement from the 1950s through the 1980s,*

p. 187.

[66]   Carson, *In Struggle: SNCC and the Black Awakening of the 1960s*, p. 117.

[67]   Ibid.

[68]   Bruce Watson, *Freedom Summer: The Savage Season That Made Mississippi Burn and Made America a Democracy* (New York: Viking Penguin, 2010), p. 215.

[69]   Friedland, *Lift Up Your Voice Like a Trumpet: White Clergy and the Civil Rights and Antiwar Movements, 1954–1973*, p. 133.

[70]   Leonard, *Call to Selma: Eighteen Days of Witness*, p. 106.

[71]   Zellner, *The Wrong Side of Murder Creek: A White Southerner in the Freedom Movement*, p. 142.

[72]   Ibid., 141.

[73]   Constance Curry, *Deep in Our Hearts: Nine White Women in the Freedom Movement* (Athens, GA: University of Georgia Press, 2000), p. 342.

[74]   Ibid., p. 355.

[75]   Ibid., p. 368.

[76]   Justine Priestley, *By Gertrude Wilson: Dispatches of the 1960s, From a White Writer in a Black World* (Edgartown, MA: Vineyard Stories, 2005), pp. 139*ff.*

[77]   Andrew Young, *An Easy Burden: The Civil Rights Movement and the Transformation of America* (New York: HarperCollins Publishers, Inc., 1996), p. 331.

[78]   Harry Belafonte, *My Song: A Memoir* (New York: Alfred A. Knopf, 2011), pp. 3–11.

[79]   Lewis, *Walking with the Wind: A Memoir of the Movement*, p. 359.

[80]   Fager, *Selma 1965*, p. 159.

[81]   King, *My Life with Martin Luther King, Jr.*, p. 247.

[82]   Eagles, *Outside Agitator: Jon Daniels and the Civil Rights*

Movement in Alabama, p. 42.

83 Priestley, *By Gertrude Wilson: Dispatches of the 1960s, From a White Writer in a Black World*, p. 143.

84 Branch, *At Canaan's Edge: America in the King Years 1965–68*, pp. 159–160.

85 Lewis, *Walking with the Wind: A Memoir of the Movement*, p. 360.

86 King, *My Life with Martin Luther King, Jr.*, p. 249.

87 Gary May, *The Informant: The FBI, the Ku Klux Klan and the Murder of Viola Liuzzo* (New Haven, CT: Yale University Press, 2005), p. 144.

88 Ibid., pp. 147–150.

89 *The Selma-Times Journal*, March 26, 1965.

90 Lewis, *Walking with the Wind: A Memoir of the Movement*, p. 361.

91 Shattuck, *Episcopalians and Race: Civil War to Civil Rights*, p. 154.

92 Eagles, *Outside Agitator: Jon Daniels and the Civil Rights Movement in Alabama*, p. 47.

93 Ibid., p. 50.

94 Ibid., p. 82.

95 Ibid., p. 87.

96 *The New York Times*, August 23, 1965.

97 Malcolm Boyd, *As I Live and Breathe: Stages of an Autobiography* (New York: Random House, Inc. 1965), p. 156.

98 *Southern Courier*, August 28–29, 1965.

99 Carmichael, *Ready for Revolution: The Life and Struggles of Stokely Carmichael*, p. 467.

100 Hampton and Fayer, *Voices of Freedom: An Oral History of the Civil Rights Movement from the 1950s through the 1980s*, p. 273.

[101]   Carmichael, *Ready for Revolution: The Life and Struggles of Stokely Carmichael*, p. 466.

[102]   Jack Nelson, *Scoop: The Evolution of a Southern Reporter* (Jackson, MS: University of Mississippi Press, 2013), p. 142.

[103]   *The New York Times*, August 23, 1965.

[104]   Carmichael, *Ready for Revolution: The Life and Struggles of Stokely Carmichael*, pp. 470–471.

[105]   Carson, *In Struggle: SNCC and the Black Awakening of the 1960s*, p. 196.

[106]   *The New York Times*, August 5, 1966.

[107]   Peniel E. Joseph, *Dark Days, Bright Nights: From Black Power to Barack Obama* (Philadelphia: Basic Civitas Books, 2010), p. 125.

[108]   James T. Patterson, *The Eve of Destruction: How 1965 Transformed America* (New York: Basic Books, 2012), p. 240.

[109]   Joseph, Dark Days, *Bright Nights: From Black Power to Barack Obama*, p. 130.

[110]   Dan T. Carter, *The Politics of Rage: George Wallace, the Origins of the New Conservatism, and the Transformation of American Politics* (New York: Simon & Schuster, 1995), p. 256.

[111]   Lewis, *Walking with the Wind: A Memoir of the Movement*, pp. 361–362.

CPSIA information can be obtained at www.ICGtesting.com
Printed in the USA
LVOW08s1338311013

359465LV00001B/41/P